Self and Soul

More praise for Self and Soul

Lorraine Ash writes eloquently and with arresting honesty. Her journey illuminates those human sensibilities that best bring us into a working relationship with the wholeness-making energies of god.

— Robert C. Fuller, Ph.D.
Author, *Spiritual, But Not Religious:*
Understanding Unchurched American Religion

Self and Soul is the interior story of a surprisingly dramatic spiritual journey that masterfully illustrates abstract concepts such as despair and peace in vivid concrete details.

— Pat Carr
Author, *The Women in the Mirror*
and *One Page at a Time: On a Writing Life*

Lorraine Ash moves us from the Catholicism of her youth into her search for the divine promised land. On the journey she gently winds her way back to its true place — the sacred home within. Her writing enchants and uplifts, and her noble heart will win yours.

— Julie Bond Genovese
Author, *Nothing Short of Joy*

Once again Lorraine Ash takes us on a quiet journey into the divine depths of the soul. This book lingers in the heart and gives us permission to mine the meaning in our own hidden heartbreaks and private joys.

—Julie Lange
(www.ravensdrum.com)
Author, *Life Between Falls:*
A Travelogue Through Grief and the Unexpected

This is riveting reading that offers lucid and deeply meaningful descriptions for experiences and intuitions that previously seemed indescribable.

—John E. Welshons
(www.onesoulonelove.com)
Author, *One Soul, One Love, One Heart*
and *Awakening from Grief*

Self and Soul

On Creating a Meaningful Life

Lorraine Ash

Foreword by Joseph Dispenza

C△PE
HOUSE
CAPE HOUSE BOOKS
ALLENDALE, NEW JERSEY

SELF AND SOUL
On Creating a Meaningful Life

Copyright © 2012 Lorraine Ash

ISBN-10: 1-939129-00-1
ISBN-13: 978-1-939129-00-0

Cape House Books™
PO Box 200
Allendale, NJ 07401-0200

www.CapeHouseBooks.com

Cover and book design by Bill Ash

Publisher's Cataloging Information

Ash, Lorraine.
Self and Soul: On Creating a Meaningful Life/ by Lorraine Ash;
Foreword by Joseph Dispenza. 1st ed.

     p. cm.

ISBN-10: 1-939129-00-1
ISBN-13: 978-1-939129-00-0

1. Spiritual life — healing aspects. 2. Spiritual growth — women.
3. Bereavement — spiritual aspects. 4. Spiritual healing — addiction.
5. Writing — inspiration. 6. Healing — spiritual aspects.
7. Addiction — spiritual healing. 8. Spirituality — recovery.

BM645.L7K87 2010
158.120802-dc22

                                                    12346978610

                        1 2 3 4 5 6 7 8 9 10

For Bill

"Live the questions now. Perhaps you will then gradually, without noticing it, live along some distant day into the answer."
— Rainer Maria Rilke

"Who looks outside, dreams; who looks inside, awakes."
— Carl Jung

Contents

Foreword

The Seeker archetype carries within it a trap that most of us notice only after we have gone intensely into our own search, out to vast expanses and down to profound depths. Some sincere seekers never appear to see the trap—and often fall through it on a downward spiral to a kind of seeker's hell.

In the Medieval story of the Holy Grail, popularized most recently by *The Da Vinci Code* and its imitators, the archetype emerges in its full glory. The Grail was said to be the cup of the Last Supper and at the Crucifixion to have received blood flowing from Christ's side. It was taken to Britain by a disciple, the shadowy Joseph of Arimathea, where it lay hidden for centuries.

After the fall of the Roman Empire, the search for the sacred vessel became the principal quest of the knights of King Arthur. It was believed to be kept in a mysterious castle surrounded by a wasteland and guarded by a custodian called the Fisher King, who suffered from a wound that would not heal. His recovery and the renewal of the blighted lands depended upon the successful completion of the quest.

Many knights went out to seek the Grail—myths and fairytales of the Middle Ages are filled with references to knights who took up the quest. Most of the legends trace the journey of Sir Percival, who, because of his personal purity and dedication to self-knowledge, was considered the perfect candidate for finding the Grail. The story goes that he spent years in the search, traveling through several countries, and encountering many obstacles. Finally, weary and discouraged, he sat down exhausted under a tree. After some time, he looked up, and there was the Grail, caught in the branches of the tree.

The story of Percival's search for the Grail is about the eternal yearning we have to know more about ourselves. We appear to be hardwired for self-discovery. We go out and try to find everything we can about ourselves—who we are, where we came from, why we are here, where we are going. In the end, we come back to ourselves, to the place inside where the solutions to our personal puzzles reside.

Percival was looking for the Grail, the answer to all life's questions, the ultimate healing, and the key to happiness. He found it in the most unexpected place: right where he was. The search for happiness always ends when we realize that we already have happiness in the moment, if we will only recognize it.

For the Seeker, there must be an end to the search; if not, she just keeps on searching, even when there is nothing to find. That is the trap within the archetype.

This book is about what happens when we stop looking — for happiness, for meaning, for purpose, for answers, for the causes of our content or discontent. It is a brave spiritual memoir that gathers lessons together in the manner of the true Seeker, out of all that is encountered on the path of life, from the tragedy of an infant death and the strictures of growing up in a rule-bound religion to encounters with invaluable teachers, whether as people or situations.

Lorraine Ash has given us here a plan for connection to the Divine, a way to have a one-on-one relationship with the Source, from her own rich life experiences. Good memoir is supposed to instruct us — good spiritual memoir is supposed to lead us to spiritual truth. You will find that here, as Percival found the Grail, when he finally was done with the search.

—Joseph Dispenza
www.lifepathretreats.com

Joseph Dispenza is the author of *God On Your Own: Finding a Spiritual Path Outside Religion* and *The Way of the Traveler,* and many other books about leading a higher quality of life. He is the founder of LifePath Retreats in San Miguel de Allende, Mexico.

Self and Soul

The paradox of loss

Voicelessness

The Second Ecumenical Council of the Vatican opened three years after I was born. So I grew up inside a controversy that would help shape my life — whether it was best to speak to God in English or Latin. The former, some said, was a natural way and people could follow the Mass better in their native language. But the latter, others held, embodied the mysteries of faith and invoked an ancient awe-inspiring tradition including cathedrals, incense and Gregorian chants.

I learned and liked both. Immediately I confess to preferring the Latin, a fact that would make

Sister Aurea, my high school Latin teacher, proud. I was elected treasurer of the National Latin Honor Society in my junior year, which meant I could don a toga, braid garlands into my hair and carry a scroll while participating in assemblies. In those days members of the Latin honor society were easy to spot.

These days I invoke my now-limited Latin at dire times. When I'm called back for a diagnostic mammogram, for instance, or when I'm climbing a cliff in Maine and looking down at treetops. Then the *In nomine patri et fili et spiritus sanctus* comes rolling out.

Either way, the main thing is that my prayers (English or Latin), which is to say the actual words that flew up to the invisible castle of Catholicism, were not written by me. They were written for me. Whatever the language, the words were put in my mouth. Back in the '60s and '70s this thought did not occur to any of us (as far as I know). Certainly not to me, the smallest, thinnest and usually first person in any church processional. Nor to any of the uniformed classmates I led, right back to the tallest and last girl. God, I presumed, must like the symmetry of our lines, or, more probably, the discipline required to create them. At least it showed some care in the way we presented ourselves. We must prepare to meet God, I learned, not unlike the way my father prepared his law cases, the way my Italian grandmother ironed the pleats in my uniforms or the way I prepared my Latin homework, spreading conjugations and declensions over the dining room table. So many rules to speak the language of God. So much to know before we dare utter a word.

Even today the prayers I was handed throughout my youth, for the purpose of saying or singing, run through my mind. One raw December evening in the church, the choir, including me among the first sopranos, split itself into three-part harmony as we rehearsed, *Adeste fidelis, laeti triumphantes, venite, venite in Bethlehem. Oh come all ye faithful, joyful and triumphant. Come ye, oh come ye, to Bethlehem.* When I was older, in sixth grade, and preparing for the sacrament of Confirmation and the coming of the bishop who officiated, I memorized reams of questions and answers. Both were furnished — my questions, God's answers. My classmates and I rehearsed ceremonies. At one point we filed out of pews so that we knelt, ready to be individually blessed, on cue, in front of the bishop, each of us with a sponsor standing behind us. My sponsor, my cousin Kathy, waited patiently for our turn, her hand resting on my shoulder. At the end we filed out and sang, *I'm a soldier in Christ's army, Confirmation made it so.* We were troops headed into the battle of life.

During my college years I was setting up the guitars and sound system on the altar of the same church with the parish music ministry one Sunday morning, in preparation for our singing at the 11 o'clock mass, as usual. The priest who was to celebrate Mass that day asked me and the other female musician to step down. He had a question.

"Are either of you at the time of the month?" he asked.

"Yes," I said. His expression darkened.

"You cannot perform today, I am sorry."

"Why not?"

"Your presence defiles the altar."

There were many currents in the waters of Catholicism during those Vatican II transition years. Somehow, in enhancing the communal experience of prayer, it seemed the personal, mystical dimension of the religion was downplayed, perhaps unintentionally. My unsanctioned quest for a direct experience of God was not new in the Catholic world. Indeed it was very old and, though it felt dangerous to me to pursue my longings and spiritual adventures, the powerful repercussions I encountered were mild compared to those of, say, the Spirituali, sixteenth-century Catholic reformers who lived during the Inquisition. The day the priest spoke to me I did step off the altar and that was that. In the years that followed I kept playing with the guitar group, which rehearsed a hundred or more songs and offered them in harmony. Our music drew many people to the church.

But all was not well within me. After I was out of college and graduate school, I enrolled in a years-long night course of study at a metaphysical center. We studied ancient texts, the origins and development of belief systems, the commonality among religions. As I left for class one evening, my Catholic father rustled his newspaper and, without making eye contact, asked, "Why go? Is their god any better than ours?"

The story stops

To this day I cannot get enough of the Buddhist sutras, the Bible or the Hindu Vedas. What we allow in our minds is what is there to process. So, when the details of some great trauma, loss or disappointment storm the doors of our consciousness, they are greeted by the ancient teachings. Words of wisdom have a way of weaving around our emotional pain, helping us come to terms with what was previously inconceivable — sometimes even moments before.

But the words, however helpful, are not the Creator himself. At least in my experience, it is relatively easy to ingest a truth. Open-mindedness and time are all that is required. But to come soul to soul with God requires relationship and a willingness to walk through the stories of our lives and into His arms. All our stories can be such avenues to the divine, or all stories can be prisons, depending on the consciousness of the person. When I think of my life I envision a home free-floating in a black cosmic field of stars. Since I live in a linear world, my story has a beginning, a time when I had to walk through the front door of the home. Inside, the story rages, ebbs and flows, and I change it with my responses to what happens. From the inside, it can seem that God is out there in the formless, remote cosmic field and that I must do something to get to Him. It is easy to think that first I must prepare myself to meet God, which requires a story in which I ready myself, perhaps even elaborately. Or perhaps I imagine I must first build a spacecraft sturdy enough to make the trip to divinity, and that, too, requires a story. A story of building. The most useful change I can create inside the home, though, is one of consciousness. It comes when I realize my real home *is* the great cosmic field that surrounds the structure of my life, when I take the time to focus my gaze out any window and remind myself my life and story are part of the greater mystery. No traveling required. I'm already there. Those are times all stories stop and enlightenment begins. Peace does not have to do with finding the right story but by stopping stories, by contemplating the mystery in silence and listening to the replies in the stillness of my heart. But stories can go on for years. Some are so large, complicated and old — even intergenerational — that it is easy to forget they are stories at all.

For forty years I lived inside the same story of seeking and struggling. The walls of the house of my story were built on long-tended family beliefs: Those who do good, get good. God takes care of true believers. Fate smiles upon the virtuous. Those walls detonated on June 2, 1999, the night I met God as I lay in an intensive care unit at a state-of-the-art university hospital mere miles from New York City. It was dark, but the time of day was irrelevant. There was no window in the room where I lay, hooked up to catheters, IV drips of antibiotics running through my veins, holding in one hand a contraption I could press for more morphine. In the wee hours of that morning I had had a C-section. The corpse of my sweet daughter, Victoria Helen, had been cut out of me as I lay on an operating table, my arms outstretched on either side of me, looking up into the eyes of a masked anesthesiologist.

"Are you all right?" he asked me.

"Yes," I said.

I had never been less all right. At my side was my husband, ever kind, as bewildered as I at what we had learned hours earlier: Our daughter had died in utero. Silently. Without warning. I was forty-two weeks pregnant, finishing a perfect pregnancy. We had started the day excited, happy, in our doctor's office across the street from the hospital. He had held his Doppler to my stomach and said, "I can't find a heartbeat." All the king's horses and all the hospital's fancy equipment could not find, or retrieve, that precious heartbeat. In the maternal fetal medicine department a nurse had tried to find the elusive beating, which had been strong all those nine months. She looked and she listened. She could not find it, she said.

"So my daughter is dead?" I asked.

"Yes."

There were only the three of us in the huge room, which was decorated with collages of babies. Beautiful shiny faces smiling at us. They had all lived, each and every one. But my Victoria Helen had slipped away.

"I will leave you with some forms to fill out," the nurse continued. She handed my husband sheets attached to a clipboard and left the room. My husband took the papers and let out an ungodly wail. To this day I have not heard such a sound come from a human being. Tears poured from his eyes.

We had come to think of our daughter's birth as destined since we conceived her, our first and only child, on the first try when I was thirty-nine. But our "Sweetlet," as we affectionately called her, was dead. There I was, stroking my husband's back, kissing his head, watching the faces of all the babies on the walls, stunned. For all the world, stunned.

Much later, after an autopsy, we learned a naturally occurring Group B Strep infection had seeped from my vagina to my uterus, probably through some microscopic tear, causing Victoria Helen to aspirate meconium and quietly die. After the C-section I awakened with a 103-degree fever. I had the infection, and the fight of my life, on my hands. The fever stayed with me two weeks until, finally, my doctor discovered the pocket where the infection still resided and removed it.

But as the night of June 2 turned into the morning of June 3, the cause of the fever remained unknown. My body was on fire, as I soaked through gown after hospital gown, enduring the agony of being touched, moved and changed. My intestines stopped working. I had no strength. I had used all my strength and I had lost. What losses. My daughter. My health. Almost my life.

I already missed the feeling of my daughter's body inside me. She had to have gone somewhere. I believed she went to God. Yet she seemed still with me, and in that tomblike night, with the lights flashing and machines beeping and the sweat pouring off me and my husband sitting in a chair at the foot of my bed reassuringly holding my feet, so did God. My mind compressed my whole life and the universe in flashes: I was sitting on a chair in my living room a week earlier, my palm stroking my big belly. Then I was a girl, falling asleep under fresh sheets my mother had dried in the clear New Jersey breezes out on the line as, downstairs, my Italian relatives laughed and talked and drank coffee. A young woman, I was on the Shore Path in Bar Harbor, Maine, sitting on a wall and looking out over Frenchman's Bay, the wind in my hair, as my husband scrambled on the rocks below and looked up to wave and smile. Wind and fresh air, mothers and daughters, lineages and love.

I had just lost my place in this chain of passing down, and my daughter had gone to God, which I implored in the middle of the night. My mind flashed to the cosmos, to that starry black field, to a Native American dance I had once seen performed under a bright afternoon sun, to my husband and me sitting on our porch drinking my homemade lemonade. The world had collapsed, gone out of linear order until, somehow, I grasped that my soul, having escaped the world of contained expectation I had constructed, was flying free for a time, showing me what mattered. The scenes surprised me. They were simple. They contained elements of nature and freedom and love enjoyed and appreciated in the moment. My Victoria Helen had slipped, God seemed to tell me, into one of these scenes. For eternity. Forever, she was in the wind, the love, the smile, the sheets, the lemonade, the stars, the dance, the ocean. These were not the scenes my mind would have chosen as the pinnacles of my life, but my mind was not doing the choosing. My soul was. At first it seemed my soul held my daughter as it simultaneously touched me with one angelic hand and God with the other.

Then I suddenly realized my whole life, and my daughter, were inside God. We were part of His great creative force.

In that moment I felt God within me and surrounding the bed. I felt God holding me and Victoria. I went to sleep, the voice of a nurse saying something, the warmth of Bill's hands on my feet. Something had happened to all of us and it was all right. So a hospital room, I learned, can be a cathedral, a place for a transcendental moment.

Bill and I once stayed at a lightkeeper's house on Isle au Haut, an island off the coast of Maine with no electricity. At night the light's rotating light would periodically color the dining room of our inn, casting a red sheen over all the guests. In the morning we would hike into the national park and once encountered a field of trees so magnificent I am sure it will come to mind in my final days when my life flashes before me again. The trees were mighty monuments. I looked up at the sunlight streaming through them and onto the forest floor, reflecting greens in so many hues it forced me to smile. The tops of the trees, so high, arced to form a kind of ceiling over the meadow below. A cathedral right there in nature. An honest-to-God cathedral. *The world is a cathedral*, I thought. *I am a cathedral.* Everything and everyone is a dwelling place for God.

Instantly and imperceptibly, I dropped my faith in God, replacing it with a knowledge of God and I understood even my earliest searching instinct for what it was—not a human impulse but a divine spark trying to awaken itself.

The autumn after Victoria Helen died Bill and I returned to the Shore Path in Bar Harbor. He scrambled down below as I walked with my friend Mark on the path above.

"Why do you think it happened?" he asked.

"I don't know," I said, realizing that for the first time I accepted that answer as a part of life and did not resist it as a failure or embrace it as a challenge. Some things are not knowable. Though I still have stressful days in my professional and personal life, it is mainly the stress of frustration, logistics, and limited resources. It is not the old existential stress, that old wondering where I fit into the world. To this day I marvel that my daughter had to slip out of the physical world before I realized where both of us, all of us, fit into it.

What struck me, too, about Mark's question was the use of the word "you." Whoever I was, I had changed. Perhaps so much that I was now someone different. Before Victoria's death I had been so busy in the world. But *who* was busy? Who was I? Perhaps before Victoria, the world had formed me too much. Perhaps I had poured too much of my energy into prescribed molds of behaviors, activities and expectations.

But afterwards I felt the stirrings of a new calling: To write words that cracked open the essence of life. To make the world see stillbirth and the voiceless babies it claims, to expand the meaning of motherhood, to change the paradigm of living the good life, to open new doors of spirituality that make allowance for an individual experience of God. Because I had changed, everything else did, too. Anaïs Nin said it best, "We don't see things as they are, we see things as we are."

For most of my adult life I had accompanied my mother whenever she visited the cemetery where many of her ancestors are buried, going back to her grandmother, Vittoria. Some version of this name, Italian or American, runs through both sides of my family, which is how my husband and I came to name our daughter Victoria. Every Easter, every Christmas, my mother and I would go through the ritual at the cemetery. We would visit the relatives, starting with my grandparents, interred in a mausoleum. We would find a caretaker who would roll a ladder to the site so I could climb up and place fresh flowers in front of my grandparents' names, Nina Raccagni Sonzogni and Taddeo Sonzogni. After saying prayers, shedding tears and reminiscing, I drove us down a pastoral hill to the grave of my Aunt Olga, who was a nurse who had loved and nurtured me in my girlhood. It was Olga who accompanied my frightened mother to the hospital when she gave birth to me.

Close to Olga was Zia Esther (my grandmother's sister) and Zio Primo, both superb cooks. Primo had stowed away to America on a ship; in midlife, the couple ran a boardinghouse on a farm in Chester, New York, where dozens of family members would gather on weekends for an afternoon in the fresh air. The women would carry out large bowls of steaming pasta with homemade sauce and trays of veal cutlet parmigiana and scrumptious hot Italian bread, all prepared by Esther and Primo. The food would be placed between clear-glass carafes of red wine on long tables in an open field. The backdrop for the feast, filled with laughter, storytelling and newsy chatting, was a wide-open countryside, green as far as the eye could see.

We brought flowers to Esther and Primo in their final resting place, got back in the car and drove to where Eduardo and Vittoria (my grandmother's mother) were buried, side by side. There my mother would tell me the story about how she had gone to Eduardo's funeral when she was a girl. He was laid out in his home, as was the custom in those days. A persistent fly buzzed around his face, landing from time to time on his forehead. The fly mesmerized my mother, leaving an indelible memory. Then she went on: When she was a girl she and my grandmother would visit the cemetery and leave flowers as organ music was piped over the whole scene.

Farther down the hill, my Great Aunt Virginia was buried with my Great Uncle Willie (my grandfather's brother). The two had worked with their father for a long time, both absorbing classical training, Italian style, in the art of tiling. The morning after my eighth-grade graduation party, my family, including my grandfather, was sitting at the kitchen table in my house eating lunch, when the phone rang. My mother answered and handed the phone to my grandfather. He put the phone to his ear and listened. "Thank you," he said, before handing the phone back to my mother. "Willie's dead," he said. Great Uncle Willie had died suddenly of an aneurysm. My grandfather's head drooped down and his shoulders shook. He was crying for Willie. All those years together. Done.

At the base of the hill, my mother and I brought flowers to Olga's parents—Caesarina (another sister of my grandmother after whom Bill and I would have named a second daughter, if we had had one) and her husband, John. Caesarina died very young, of a heart condition. John lived a long time, beyond the point his memory could carry him.

This cemetery cloaked me in history, made me proud to be part of a strong tribe of ancestors who clearly had a lust for living and an artistic streak that manifested in colorful meals and mosaic masterpieces. They had long and often difficult stories, all of them, but they had kept passing down the love and the lust and the color. A few years after

Victoria died, I no longer could perform this ritual with my mother. It made me feel too sharply the great break in the chain that my own experience represented. I possess their lust and colorful creativity — manifesting, in my case, on the page and in the kitchen — but I feel no genetic flow into the future. I used to, but one day it stopped. Like a drained stream, it simply ended. There is poignant sadness in the stopping. However, one inherits what one inherits — the good, the brilliant, the happy, the difficult and the impossible — and one spins of it the most bright golden thing possible.

All the time I meet people who tell me the best part of their lives is having children, raising them, watching them grow, and I can only imagine the excitement of seeing a progeny develop, the satisfaction of seeing one's own child reach her hand into the future and grasp it. People believe in the future, especially when the present is lacking, and that is a very good thing.

But none of this applies to me, standing as I do on a different brink. My life used to divide into a past of inherited legacies, a present of lack and a future of expectation. Spiritually, it divided into two places — where I was and where God was — and the search for the promised land seemed endless. No more. The circumstances of my life now have me looking out the windows of my cosmic house and the stories I live are the stories I write for myself. It is good not to walk a path forged by the tribe but rather our own. We cannot help but walk with our ancestors, but we also always walk with our one common ancestor — God.

I no longer listen to those who (still) exclaim to me that it is a shame my life has become something lesser than it could have been, that it is a shame I am not raising my daughter. To inhabit such a space I would have to accept that the bounds of physical limitations determine my fate. To an extent, they do. They determine my biological fate. But, no matter what happens to any of us in this regard, there is always a divine fate to which we are called. Not one life on this planet is wasted. Not for one moment. Each of us stands on some patch of land in this world, and no matter where it is, or how small or how remote, every patch is fertile ground ready to accept whatever meaning we plant there. It is not until we learn this, as a race, that we will tread on each other's patches with respect and the world community will know peace.

Jelaluddin Rumi, the thirteenth-century mystic poet, wrote the oft-cited passage, "Out beyond ideas of wrongdoing and rightdoing, there is a field. I'll meet you there." This is the inner field on which each of us meets God. The voice of an uninterpreted, pure God ready to hold a unique, divine conversation with each of His creations. I still cannot answer Mark's question: "Why do you think it happened?" The question may be, "Why does any loss happen?" By definition, a loss is a stripping away, layer by layer, that is paradoxical. In my case, first there was the death of my daughter. As I processed her loss, my outer mission (if you will) grew. I wrote, I read from my book, I spoke with many bereaved mothers, I taught writing-to-heal workshops, and the rest of my journalistic career deepened. On the surface, all that activity may look like an adding of roles and complexity. But through this time my inner life became more and more a matter of subtracting and simplifying. All the outer actions manifested a single spiritual odyssey.

After Victoria died, I left my role as newspaper editor to embrace fully my role as writer, so I could spend all my time doing what I love best. Inwardly, I detached from relationships that were energetic cesspools, relationships that promised reward but only by embracing some negative dynamic. I stopped teaching people who did not want to be taught. I ceased indulging in spiritualities of the marketplace that require a gold rush for endless acquisitions of knowledge nuggets, all attached to promises of peace and wisdom. These dams removed, insights birthed in the inner waters of my spirit flowed from my pen.

Loss is paradoxical because it can take with it needless psychic debris and layers of struggle, leaving us ultimately in the sole company of what we can never lose—God. This is how I found my voice at last—by talking to God, directly. This is when I found the words that allowed me entrance into the sacristy of my own mind and heart. Now I speak to God but not as a child talks to an adult. Not through prayers penned by some third party. Not as an intellectual asking for proof or a desperate person wanting a favor. But as one soul talking to the Great Soul and listening, through the world around me and in the whispers of my mind, for a reply.

The stripping away that the death of my daughter put into motion lead to a profound connection with life in its essence. The divine does permeate this world in order to hold and teach us. Alleluia.

The dark ages

Days of discontent

Whether I ever would have found spiritual freedom without the trauma of my outer life, I will never know. I am still astonished, though, at how the pain of loss and tragedy was able to so thoroughly re-baptize me. So intimate and complete was it that my very cells and synapses seemed to change the way they vibrated and connected within me. I figured there was an intelligence at work. I let it happen and, after a time, I trusted that intelligence and called it God.

Certainly the years of work I had done on myself before Victoria's death already had helped me question my own conditioning. In retrospect, I understand they helped me develop the kind of resilient mind that could process change. What wondrous years they were. Back in the days I took metaphysics courses at night, I also saw a Jungian therapist. In her office was a small low altar bearing statues of different god images, including Ganesh, a deity with an elephant's head from the pantheon of Hinduism, a monotheistic religion that represents different aspects of consciousness with different figures. Ganesh is the Remover of Obstacles. Perfect for a therapist's office. He also is Lord of Beginnings. Equally suitable. I told the therapist about my father's comment when I started the metaphysics classes: "Why go? Is their god any better than ours?"

"There is only one God," Jennifer said, "but the different religions allow for different divine personalities since people all have different personalities. A person who does not relate to God, the judgmental father, cannot talk to such a being. But he can talk to another face of God."

Not another God. Another face of God. God has many faces. As Seneca, the ancient Roman philosopher, wrote, "*Facilius enim per partes in cognitionem totius adducimur.*" Or, we are more easily led, part by part, to an understanding of the whole. After this realization, the mosaic of belief, laid so painstakingly inside me by others, piece by piece, slightly shifted. The symmetry was no longer perfectly

Catholic. I thought of one of the pictorial mosaics my grandfather tiled on the ceilings of holy places and how he would set a section in place, come down off his scaffolding to stand on the floor and look up to study what he had done. Eventually he shook his head. Then he climbed up once more and took down some tiles. He was trying to make it perfect; I was trying to make my inner mosaic more imperfect, which is to say less institutionally correct and more personal. The idea of shooting for imperfection was foreign to me, though the definition of "perfection" was becoming more slippery.

The therapist had mentioned a person who cannot talk to a judgmental, paternal face of God. Had I ever spoken to even one face of God without pre-written aids, some of them formulated centuries before I was born? Or had I only spoken at God? That God would be interested in having me talk to Him, rather than just affirm or worship Him, had not occurred to me. The thought was so revolutionary, it astonished me. I was not alone, I would learn over and over again. Once I attended a lecture by a holistic healer who suggested that talking to God is an essential part of personal peace and healing. A sixty-something successful businesswoman struggling with stress and fatigue was so baffled by the statement that she asked, "How in the world do you do *that*?"

In the years of therapy I tested what was then a new idea. The mosaic had slipped, after all, and pieces started falling out, which was good. Mythologist Joseph Campbell said, "If you make all your choices according to the dictates of the Catholic Church, what is the difference between you and the Catholic Church?" Substitute any system of belief for Catholicism, of course. I wanted to *feel* a mosaic inside me that I could challenge and change. I wanted it to shine like a lunar orb and cast its ethereal light over my inner life. I wanted it to animate me.

So I tested the idea of having a one-on-one relationship with God. Next door to the weekly newspaper where I was beginning my journalism career as a reporter was a greasy spoon luncheonette run by a Greek man and his common law wife. Four of us gathered for lunches at the place. In addition to me, there was an agnostic male editor, Jewish by upbringing. There also was a Catholic male editor who believed intently that the Catholic heavenly world was completely superimposed over this one. (One day a mother who was living in her car with her child came to the newspaper looking for help. A few of us gave her money for the night and linked her with a homeless shelter and a couple of social agencies. When she drove off, I said, "Poor woman." The Catholic editor looked at me. "That was no woman," he said. "She was Jesus in disguise. That was a test." The Benedictines greet and treat everyone *as if* they were Christ, a laudable practice sans the idea of a test.) Also in our foursome was a middle-aged Protestant editor. Yankee, practical, the kind of woman who, if you were hungry, would sit you at her table and serve you a meal whether you were a deity or a mortal and no matter what you believed.

All of us delved into the topic of God. The agnostic would say, "I hope there is something more to life than getting up and going to work, quitting at the end of the day, having dinner, going to sleep and doing it all over again. I hope there is some kind of reason and maybe that's God."

"Reason!" the Catholic editor would rail. "God is a matter of faith, and we all had better believe or be struck down." I would reply that perhaps God doesn't want to smite us from the outside but talk to us on the inside.

"Blasphemy," the Catholic would reply, flying in the face of a long Christian mystical tradition including Saint Augustine, Saint Nicephorus the Solitary, Hildegard of Bingen, Saint Francis of Assisi, Meister Eckhart, Julian of Norwich, Saint Teresa of Avila, Saint Catherine of Siena, Saint John of the Cross, and Teilhard de Chardin. "Who are you that God would live in you? What makes you so special? Forget that and believe in God the father."

I had tried, of course, to believe as he did but was still left discontent and searching. "Why?" I asked.

The blood drained from the Catholic editor's face and he put down his hamburger. "Why?" he asked. "Because if you don't, you're going to hell, that's why."

Unable to help herself, a wide smile curved the lips of the Protestant as she glanced at the editor. "How do you know?"

Incredulous, he looked at her, "I don't mean to offend, but it's very well known. The Church has been teaching it for years."

"But how do you know the Church is right?" the Protestant editor asked. She popped a french fry into her mouth. "We're journalists, you know. We ask questions for a living. How do you know your church is right, and how does your church arrive at that conclusion in the first place?"

"The Church is beyond the scope of being questioned."

"Says who?" asked the Protestant.

"Says the Church."

"Would you accept that from a political party?" she asked.

"Politics is about people," he said. "Religion is about God."

"Is it?" the Protestant asked.

I relayed these talks to my agnostic boyfriend at the time.

"I've been thinking about divine sparks," he said one night, echoing a theme from one of the metaphysical classes. "Maybe we do all have one, and I sure love yours."

We married in the summer of 1989, the questions still unsettled but I, at least, feeling more inner luminosity. The mystery was awakening in me as the sterility of certainty died. If there was nothing of the divine for me to find, explore and activate within myself, what was my purpose in being alive? Though my journalism career kept going and going, the inner mosaic of discontent drew me into another kind of writing. Writing as an art of self-creation. I wrote to call a new me into being and contribute to the literature of the self. When something happened to or around me, I evaluated it in terms of what it taught me about life, God and myself. Sometimes an experience changed or tweaked a belief or caused me to act in a new way. I wondered if the process could be a microcosm of what was happening all the time everywhere. Or, perhaps, what was supposed to be happening.

Is the whole universe a series of concentric circles of creation? God within interacting with God without? The best way to know, I figured, was to ask God. But that didn't happen. I didn't trust spiritual freedom yet. More slip-sliding would go on first. If it were true that the world is a testing ground, full of inner and outer land mines tended by Satan and meant to trip up any soul who doesn't tow the line, no inner impulse could be trusted. Not in what Carl Sagan once called "the demon-haunted world."

The safe way was to second-guess all emotions and thoughts, turning them over immediately to the interpretation of spiritual leaders. Safest yet was to douse all stirrings, cleanse the inside of mind and heart so as to feel nothing and be tempted by nothing. Surely such was the way to escape the tests and relax. Or was it?

But there is no turning off the emotions, mind and soul without deeming oneself dead. Surely God did not create life for us to kill it. Surely sullying up things a bit must be sacred if the sullying is for the purpose of knowing God.

Re-imagining myself as something other than a character in a world play, with the stage set as a divine obstacle course and a director, to whom I could not speak, took some doing.

Metaphysical fear

I started my journey not with the protagonist, God, but with the antagonist, Satan. It's a personality trait. I tend toward the most difficult tasks first to get them out of the way, so I can look forward to more pleasant things.

I return now to the Jungian therapist, who used, among other techniques, past life regression. Whether the dramas a patient "retrieves" in the guided meditative state of such a regression are actually past lives did and does not concern me. Perhaps the stories that present themselves are constructed of snippets from books read or films viewed by the patient. Perhaps they are pure imaginings that encase the themes and issues of the patient. Perhaps the stories somehow are plucked from the collective subconscious when needed. Or perhaps they are a combination created subconsciously. What matters to me is that in the dramas, the patient's themes and issues are given bodies and names so they can interact and in so doing expel or resolve their conflicts. A regression can extract some painful thought, memory or hurt lodged in the psyche like a stone in a kidney.

"Dream the dream onward," the therapist used to say. Jung said it, too. If we dream something dreadful, like running to the edge of a cliff and losing our balance, and then awaken, terrified, each time, we may dispel the fear by letting the story advance. At which time we may unexpectedly fly over the ravine below, or fall into an enormous soft, billowing wave of ocean that carries us somewhere we need to be, perhaps somewhere not yet in the conscious mind.

So onward I went, reclined on a futon and covered with a Navajo blanket as the therapist sat cross-legged by my side. Eyes closed, I listened to her voice bidding me to go where I needed to go. To my surprise, I saw myself descending stone steps leading down into the earth. The staircase was a huge spiral and I recalled the unsteady sensation I felt at age twelve when my father decided

the whole family, all four of us, would walk down
the Eiffel Tower. I had slung the black plastic strap
of my orange camera bag over my head and onto
my shoulder and started the trek down, almost
paralyzed at first by the discovery there was no
handrail. Slowly, I pushed myself forward. My
father and mother were bickering about the intelligence of making such a descent and my mother's
voice neared hysteria. In my mind, though, their
voices melded and receded as I made my way
down, heart pounding, Paris looming below.

The heavy stone steps of the regression were
not in open air. Thick circular rock walls encased
them. As I walked I touched the cold rock to my
right with one hand. Once I stopped to peer down
to my left and saw the center of the spiral was a
bottomless black pit. It hissed and let out the sound
of ocean spray. Torches lit the way but only illuminated the steps.

When I saw a demon crouched between two
rocks, I gave a start and drew my hand back from
the cold wall to my heart. I then saw that demons
with slimy bodies, red eyes and long tongues lived
in the walls of my story. Every step down was
tentative, but I kept walking. Like in France in real
life, there was nothing to hold for support. What
led me on was the sound of my own voice in the
upper reaches of my consciousness, at the top of the
pit, telling me to proceed. I then saw there were
doors (all closed) in the walls — doors, I instinctive-

ly knew, that led to times and places and events that had taken place in the surfacelands, the world of the living and breathing on the earth.

When I reached a certain door, I stopped walking and turned the knob. It opened into a scene from the seventeenth century where I instantly became a character in a human drama. It was as if my presence was awaited. Suddenly I was wearing a gown and comprehended my role. I was a witch already convicted by a court. Priests clutching holy books and sneering townspeople surrounded me as I was led to a stake. I was tied to the stake.

All this time, I relayed what was happening to the therapist, prompted by a question here and there and prodded onward with an occasional "How interesting," "Good" and "Do you want to go in?" At first I relayed the scenes calmly, descriptively, including when I was set on fire. I saw the bottom of my dress ablaze. But as the flames proceeded up my body, eventually encompassing the top of my head, I screamed. I screamed in the room in the pit and I screamed on the futon.

In this hellish place I had been judged, punished and expunged from the heavenly record. My soul shot out the door of that room as a blaze of white light, flew up the stone stairs and back into my consciousness as I lay under the Navajo blanket in the Jungian's office. Never in my life had I let out such uncontrollable wailing and crying. Never had

I felt such heat. My worst fears had been sealed; I was damned.

When I opened my eyes, the therapist helped me sit up, a smile on her face. "How do you feel?" she asked.

My first thought was that I had been damned, killed and expunged. My first response was to smile: It was over with.

"This is wonderful," she said. "Let's celebrate by sharing some tea." She set about making it and we sat there on that rainy morning drinking Darjeeling from ceramic mugs and talking about what happened. I loved this therapist, with her blonde hair and sincere smile, her sharp mind, her open soul. I had gone to her because of her reputation, because we both had strong minds (I figured a strong part of me should be used to rescue a weak part), because she was peaceful and flowing and also liked to write and because I wanted my face to shine with the light of contentment in hers. Mine had grown lifeless. During this era I noticed how much tinkering we women do to our faces, changing this, changing that, and I felt an inkling that we all really wanted to see changed selves reflected in our bathroom mirrors.

As the therapist and I sipped tea, we unfurled the layers of the regression. My inquiries into the nature of God and my attempts to create the shape of my own spiritual experience were blasphemous, according to what I had been taught. My soul had enacted the drama pre-set for people like me according to doctrines which had no tolerance for my kind. These dramas actually may have played out as far back as medieval times, but they are still real psychic realities in modern times.

I had been burned away, made to go poof. Yet here I was, happily drinking tea. What was going on?

"You have freed yourself," the therapist said.

"By dying?" I asked, my voice hoarse from the screaming.

"By killing off a part of yourself that you could no longer live with."

"So dying doesn't mean losing everything?"

No. It turned out to be a skill. I recalled my metaphysics teacher talking about the importance of the contexts of dying. She talked about the cool, intelligent way a surgeon sets about removing a cancer. It dies, but only to save the whole body. Now, I had learned, it is the same with the soul. What emotional violence, though. The therapist and I talked about that, too.

"If there is a virtue in violence," she said, "it is in the opportunity it gives us to reorganize ourselves."

The stained glass of my religious identity had been shattered. Once, in an old classroom at an Ivy League college at a writing conference, a novelist talked about how to make a fictional story from a nonfictional story. The latter, he said, with its facts and its order, must be smashed. Take a proverbial hammer to it, he advised. Then walk among the shards and start putting them together in new ways. That's how great fiction is written, he said. I understood. My experience had taught me, though, not to trust stories so static they can be rendered in glass at all. People rot in static stories.

If my experience, whatever it was, shattered anything, it was nothing less than my view of the cosmos, starting with that stinking pit of a hell. It was a while before I submerged myself again, but I had some related work to do in the surfacelands, the conscious world, anyway. What about Satan? I wanted to know. What kind of being would relegate itself to live in a fire pit for eternity? I understand it's *his* pit, of course, and that there is something to be said for that. But not much. This Satan is said to romp, disguised, in the surfacelands to ensnare souls and drag them down into his pit to reign over them. So, the story goes, there is an unseen world just below this one and, with a single misguided deed or one misplaced trust, we can find ourselves in it. Once I traveled to Montreal and, while strolling and chatting apres-dinner with friends the very first evening, walked unwittingly through mist into the old city. On the other side of the mist, it seemed we were in another time, another reality. I was enchanted by the dewy night air on my face, the old buildings around me. I wondered,

Is this what it is like when we move between dimensions?
Do they come up on us just like that? We stroll, we
are engaged by some new sight, we stop thinking,
we live in the moment and we are ... ensnared?
There came up that old cosmological tension again.
Is there no true relaxation in this existence? Are we
really required to be so narrow in our obedience
and delights?

But back to Satan. The therapist and I traveled
into an historical adventure, which is far less exhausting than a soul journey, and I researched the
origins of the Beast and his kingdom. The Christian
church revamped the old pagan god, Pan, to come
up with Satan. There hardly has been such a make-
over in the history of existence. Pan was known as
the "rustical god," a horned, flute-playing, sexy,
soulful male deity who ruled over the Underworld,
a place of great value because from it springs life-
sustaining flowers, greenery and crops. His Underworld was a place of health and regeneration.

The gorgeous deity of the pre-Christian Underworld is famously depicted in *Pan and Psyche*, an
1870s oil painting by Sir Edward Burne Jones which
shows Pan stopping the beautiful Psyche, then still
a mortal, from drowning herself. Psyche is despon-
dent because she let her jealous sisters talk her into
disobeying the one rule her lover, Cupid, had set
for her: she was never to gaze upon his face and
know his true identity. One night, though, at her
sisters' behest, Psyche held a light to Cupid's sleep-

ing face. He awakened when a drop of hot oil from the lamp fell on his shoulder. Rebuking her, he flew away. Psyche roamed without her lover until she came to the river, where Pan stopped her from hurting herself and bid her never to try again. In the painting he is shown with one hand gently atop her head, peering into her eyes with concern. That is how gentle Pan, the god of spring, protects and nurtures life. To torment or kill is far from the mind or mission of this nature god.

His cool, water-glazed underworld of regeneration, seeds and soil had been recast as a hell of punishment, fire and no escape. Return for a moment to a time when the world below the surface of the earth was blessed. Everything changes, doesn't it? For one thing, polar thinking—thinking along a continuum where one end is Good and the other Evil—ends. There is no continuum, just a natural circle as death and regeneration yield to one another. When polarity ends, the questions we ask ourselves change. When confronted with a phenomenon, we no longer first ask: Is this beneficent or malevolent? We instead ask: Beneficent to whom? Malevolent to whom? If there is a Lord of Lies, as Satan sometimes is called, it is easy to separate the world into Truths and Lies, identifying things as one or the other. Balderdash. The search for truth starts in a lie, and the search for a lie starts in a truth. The two are so intertwined that they cannot exist apart. Once this polarity falls, others are called into question: Births and deaths, for instance. No exclusivity there at all. A leaf dies and falls to the floor of the autumn forest, only to become mulch for a new life form.

And what of those old classic partners, virtue and vice? By what standard is virtue measured? It can be kind to kill, even good. Remember that cancer. Was Hitler a cancer on the human race? Or what of men who do distinctly non-virtuous things in the name of virtue?

Or those who are virtuous because they are afraid to be otherwise? I ponder what Satan — not Pan — would say to such a man. First, it must be admitted that Satan would not say anything. Instead he would set traps for the man, immediately making Satan a hunter and the man his prey. The man would run through the forest of his life, with some of the way dark (which he would read as evil) and some of the way open and sunlit. He would come upon pretty clearings but could not enjoy them because he would, in his well-learned paranoia, read them as a different kind of evil trap that would leave him vulnerable to the hunter's arrow. The man may then use virtue as an insurance policy, performing a good deed so God may grant the man, who is running, ever running, some favor he needed in this Satanic game of catch-and-kill. His virtue, then, because of the intent behind it, becomes something else — a strategy. What is the spiritual value of such virtue?

I ponder how Pan would treat the same man. I picture him emerging, flute in hand, from the Underworld into a pretty clearing and finding the man ensnared in his own net of confusion, fear and virtue. (It is important to say Pan finds the man in the net and does not capture him.) I imagine the horned deity approaching with a quizzical but helpful look on his face and stopping at the edge of the net when the man yells out, "Come no further!" Pan asks, "But how else may I disentangle you?" The man, convinced he knows how things are, responds by roaring some obscenity into the deity's face, to which Pan replies, "Sir, you are yelling at your own fears. There is nothing to fear from me. I see no one else about and am endeavoring to help you out of this mess. For example, that part of the rope around your neck is made of lies you have uttered to yourself. Patiently, let us call them up and understand them and they will let you go." The man roars again, saying he will not be deceived by the devil. "So then," says Pan, "will you be deceived by yourself?" "I know who I am, I protect myself!" the man replies.

At this point the deity tells the man he shall not be traveling far and that, as long as the sound of his flute can be heard, he can be summoned. Hours go by, and days, and the man occasionally hears the flute music, feeling proud because he is smart enough to realize that the sweet sound is a lure and that to succumb to it will be his end. No, he thinks, he must suffer and save himself. The poor fellow does not know how to be kind or virtuous, especially to himself. His acts of virtue may draw the praise of others, but he cannot fool himself. He knows he is, above all, afraid. But even God sees that Pan tried to help.

I should like some day to imagine a conversation between Satan and Pan. I should like to know if they are buddies, if they understand or resent each other, and whether they ever work together.

Onward I continue, though, because realizing this difference between Satan and Pan did more than sweep me free from the prison that had polarized my thinking and cut off my feeling. It challenged me to look deeply into every person, place and situation I encountered, to understand its complexity, not just to categorize it as malevolent or beneficent, right or wrong, and turn over my judgments about it to a prescribed doctrine. These powers of discernment and attention required me to make hundreds of little decisions and adjustments in my thinking and feeling and relationships with others, God and myself. This is what the Buddhists call mindfulness. My mind was never the same.

Colors of consciousness

The gloaming

If ever I doubted that each of us fertilizes the patch of land on which we stand with our own meaning and energy, it was erased in the months after Victoria's death. My soul was cast in shades of darkness in those days. Everywhere I went seemed black. If I witnessed lightheartedness, I felt certain the joy was due to the inability of those present to see the darkness so apparent to me. That is how it went until one day I was invited to a picnic in the highlands of Sussex County, New Jersey.

My cousin Christine made new potato salad and chicken salad with pecans and grapes, and the family sat under the trees in her yard. Dogs yelped and children screeched in delight on nearby properties, as the aroma of burgers cooking on summer grills wafted through the air. Nothing delighted me. Then my cousin, a glass of wine in one hand, bid me walk with her to a clearing at the end of the block. Wordlessly, we sat on a log that overlooked a valley and expansive horizon. Then an amazing thing happened. Night fell, but not suddenly like the curtain of grief. Instead, it happened slowly. A streak of violet and orange stretched across the darkening canvas of the heavens. Then pink appeared. I saw the colors as openings, piercings of consciousness, and that is the way, I decided, my darkness would lift. Never before had I watched a gloaming, though neither did I usually have such a grand natural theater in which to behold one. The sky actually spoke to me, perhaps because I had paid it attention. From that moment on everything seemed to speak to me, and I enjoyed wherever I was instead of wishing I was somewhere else, fantasizing, or replaying the past in an unforgiving, anxiety-provoking loop.

Assume for a moment we are placed wherever we stand in the world, and are not there by virtue of accident or randomness. Then there must be some meaning in our environment, and a good way to start living mindfully is to study the territory.

The effect of one person paying this close attention is staggering, even on the world stage. The oratorical and military prowess of Sir Winston S. Churchill is legendary, as are his genius as a statesman, historian and writer spanning two world wars and more. What interests me, though, is how Churchill's private life as a painter sharpened his powers of observation for all his other roles. He may have been most known for his *Finest Hour* speech before the Battle of Britain and tomes like *A History of the English-Speaking Peoples*, but his little book *Painting as a Pastime* glimpses his inner life. The Muse of Painting, as he calls it, visited him as World War I unfolded. He had left the Admiralty but remained a member of the Cabinet and War Council, powerless positions that frustrated him. After playing with a children's paint-box one Sunday in the country, he wrote, he bought everything he needed to set himself up for oil painting. The next day found him, brush poised in one hand, facing a blank canvas. Figuring an azure sky naturally required white mixed with blue, he dipped his brush accordingly and painted a small bean-sized piece of sky. As he contemplated how to proceed, the artist wife of Sir John Lavery pulled into his driveway. After she demonstrated how to paint confidently in large strokes and slashes, Churchill's painting inhibitions left him forever, and his powers of observations came alive:

One is quite astonished to find how many things there are in the landscape, and in every object in it, one never noticed before. And this is a tremendous new pleasure and interest which invests every walk or drive with an added object. So many colours in the hillside, each different in shadow and in sunlight, such brilliant reflections in the pool, each a key lower than what they repeat; such lovely lights gilding or silvering surface or outline, all tinted exquisitely with pale colour, rose, orange, green or violet. I found myself instinctively as I walked noting the tint and character of a leaf, the dreamy, purple shades of mountains, the exquisite lacery of winter branches, the dim, pale silhouettes of far horizons.

Churchill brought his artist's eye and respect for the nuances of terrains into every summit he attended and every decision he made about the battlefields of World War II. Painting taught him to respect the uniqueness of every place at home and on enemy territory. How can this aptitude not have contributed to his genius? How different would the early twenty-first century be if that same respect and attention filled every leader's eyes?

Mostly, though, we fail to notice the colors of spiritual life and bypass the many possibilities, or states of being, they suggest beyond the usual black-and-white offerings of happy or sad, rich or poor, stimulated or bored, financially successful or straining. What about abundance that is spiritual, not financial? Or a sadness overpowered by the satisfaction of helping others? A failure that makes possible some genius that follows? A success that is not financially acknowledged? A poverty tempered by hope? Where are all these states on the palette of consciousness? New identities can take root in these color states, and whole lives — vibrant, useful ones — can sprout from them, producing fruit and flowering yet again when the soul glimpses even deeper vistas of possibility. The whole process starts, though, in looking closely not only at the landscapes of a countryside but inward to places we are generally advised to avoid.

Take pain, for instance. Stephen Levine, the noted author and spiritual teacher who understands the suffering of addiction and terminal illness, has said people know little about the nature of emotional pain because they invest their energy in fleeing, not facing, it. We receive much reinforcement for the suppression, too, as shown in national statistics about mood-altering drug use.

For a time I was devoted to qigong, an ancient Chinese system of slow movements designed to promote physical and mental well-being. One movement called *The Dragon Stands Between Heaven and Earth* became my favorite. It requires standing in place, knees slightly bent, and slowly raising the arms in front of the body up to chest level. Next comes making loose fists with both hands, pointing the thumbs toward each other and then moving the arms back toward the chest. Slowly, the eyes are closed and the leader of the session directs, "Imagine you are the dragon standing between heaven and earth. Feel this power." I imagine standing inside a vertical beam of light such as that on the transporter pads of *Star Trek* episodes. On top, the beam shoots straight into the heavens, and on bottom, the beam shoots down into the earth. The qigong practitioner holds that moment for at least ten minutes. Levine might call the pose a kind of meditation, which is to him "a means to endlessness" that is all-knowing and healing. To hold the pose is an act of faith that makes it possible for heaven to send many gifts into the beam, such as sudden knowledge of a deep-seated pattern in the self, a wave of forgiveness, or the courage to act in a difficult situation.

In addition to added insight and deep calm, the qigong pose is known for promoting lowered blood pressure. So after heaven deposits inspiration into our beings, it apparently also gathers an armload of stress — the same stress cycling through the energy circuits of our bodies — and flies away with it.

Mother Earth does similarly. In the mountains of Sedona, Arizona, red rock country, I was walking with an energy healer one spring morning when he bid our small group to stop on a mesa. As I did, I surveyed the mountains around me and looked down at two small flowers growing between the rocks at my feet. Then I closed my eyes and, as the healer bid us, allowed all the negative energy to drain from me down deep into Mother Earth, into the roots of things. The earth is willing to absorb it, he said, and use it as fertilizer. The lesson: If we stay put and stay open, all aspects of where we stand reveal themselves to us. It could take an instant, an hour or a year. If we believe all of heaven and earth conspired to bring us to a given moment at a given place, then to stand there mindfully is to trust that destiny.

A misguided desire for greatness, though, compels many of us to keep moving. A young journalist I once counseled could never get her career to take off. With stars in her eyes and scenes of grandeur in her head, she never stayed in one place long. Impatient, she kept moving from newspaper to newspaper in pursuit of a big audience, a flashy story and the kind of high-level corruption that would make her famous once she revealed it. She wanted to be the Woodward or the Bernstein of her generation, or nothing at all. She wanted to write a book so it could propel her into the limelight, but she could not say on what topic. To this day, she is wandering in search of the big break. If she doesn't first change herself, however, she won't find her break because her goal is not to give herself to a story but for a story to give itself to her. Great stories appear only to those devoted to the themes and truths they encapsulate, to those who keep the vigil faithfully in all seasons and see a landscape, as Churchill would, with patient, well-trained eyes.

The young journalist fell into a culturally created chasm between ordinariness and greatness, usually presented as separate and mutually exclusive spheres of being. The gap creates wanting and desiring, states of mind our marketplace has an economic stake in perpetuating. We associate greatness with having more of something, acquiring something different or being elsewhere. In other words, we are taught that greatness, like God, is always out of reach.

Contemporary poet Lucille Clifton captures the frustration of dashed expectation in her poem, *An Ordinary Woman*, written when she was thirty-eight. She looks back to when her mother was thirty-eight and forward to when her daughters, who now "blossom and promise fruit like Afrikan trees," will be of maternal age. Finding herself in the middle, she writes she had envisioned more for her life:

> *i had not expected to be*
> *an ordinary woman.*

But ordinariness, when imbued with mindfulness, is greatness at ease with itself. Greatness has to do with discovering the depths of where we stand, wherever we stand, because all places, all states and types of being, have divinity at their core. Wherever there is divinity, there is the capacity to love, and love is the magic that, when skillfully handled, transforms us into magnificent creatures. Certainly there was nothing ordinary about Clifton's National Book Award for Poetry or her status as a two-time nominee for the Pulitzer Prize. But she did it by writing from the extraordinary truth at the center of her ordinary experience.

In a cave

In 2002 I felt a sudden and inexplicable longing to go caving. I didn't want to experience a commercial cave with displays and lit paths. I wanted a difficult cave requiring kneepads, headlamps, carabiners, rappelling into canyons, and squirming through vertical tunnels. I trust my impulses, even before I understand them. Not comprehending is charming, but also part of what makes experiences vehicles of growth. Sometimes I discover the meaning of an impulse in the middle of an experience. Many times, though, I don't get the meaning until I'm writing about it, at which point it emerges from my subconscious like a mud-caked caver in a red jumpsuit climbing out of a hole in the ground.

At first I embraced the impulse to cave as a journalistic adventure. At the time there was public discussion about closing some caves in North Jersey and New York State because too many people were going down unprepared and requiring rescue, and it is neither easy or inexpensive to transport someone with a panic attack or a broken leg up 300 feet in the dark to the surface of the earth. My husband, a skilled above-the-ground climber, immediately wanted to be part of my caving party, half out of excitement for the enterprise and half out of concern I didn't have the physical aptitude to cave safely. The day of destiny arrived one Sunday in Orange County, New York, where our small entourage, including the two of us, hiked into the woods until we reached a hole in the ground barely wider than my shoulders. I stood in the hole, my legs chilled by the cold cave air below but my upper body still baking in the harsh July sun.

I looked into the sky as I snapped on my mud gloves. Then I peered into the blackness below and turned on the lamp on my helmet. A beam showed rocks, choppy and jagged, smooth and round, small and large. The coolness moistened my face. With it came the smell of damp earth. I gripped a boulder. My gloved hand slid off the rock's muddy surface. I tried again, tried until my hand felt secure. I gripped another boulder with my other hand, sat, let go and slid down, feet first, embraced by the hardness of rock until I emerged in the Rain Room.

Water dripped down the walls and from the six-foot ceiling that arced above me. Twelve people could fit in the space. I was the fourth down in a party of eight, half pros, half first-timers. I may have been new to caving, but not to rocks. Years earlier, I'd tried rock climbing. I hadn't liked struggling in the sun to surmount a boulder, but I had liked the feel of my body on the rocks, around them, against them. I liked pushing into them until my shoulder blades glided down my back and hardened. I liked the resistance of the rocks, their age, their smell.

In the Rain Room, one caver in a blue cave suit rigged a cable ladder and rope for our next descent, a thirty-foot drop. Three of us aimed our headlamps at his hands so he could see to tie. When he finished rigging, he descended into the pitch black pit. Another caver strapped a harness onto me and latched a carabiner onto a thick loop in front of the harness.

"Red means dead," he said, as he demonstrated how to turn the biner's screw so tightly that no red thread showed. Soon the others slid into the Rain Room, too, and were harnessed. Then came the lessons:

- Keep three feet between cavers when climbing or crawling.

- If a rock loosens and starts to fall, yell "Rock!" to alert the rest of the party.

- Always keep three points of contact between your body and the rocks.

- Don't touch any rock that looks unstable.

- If you're overwhelmed or terrified, get a grip on yourself. It takes 72 hours to package an injured person and get him to the surface.

- Pay attention to the leaders.

"This is serious stuff," said the caver who had harnessed us. "Sometimes rocks move and passages collapse. It's not always safe."

I gazed into the dark pit that had engulfed the rope rigger. He certainly was right.

"Thank God I'm down here," the rope harnesser said. "I couldn't live without this."

Each of us had a reason, unarticulated but urgent, to be there.

"Don't worry. It'll be all right," said the one I already had dubbed the guardian caver. He was the coaxer and encourager.

I rappelled into the pit and followed the sound of water to the Stream Passage, where two from my party sat among boulders, as if in a meadow on a cold night. Hanging from the undersides of boulders were threads like Christmas tree tinsel. They shone, silvery and wet. "Tree roots," someone said. The very bottom of a tree. Here was the bottom of everything. The limestone walls and ceilings of the passage glimmered with water droplets that looked like stars. A closer look showed fossils embedded everywhere — imprints of ancient marine animals.

We turned left, toward the Heaven Room. My sense of time left me as I focused on rock after rock, passage after passage, tunnel after tunnel, following the cavers on our trip 160 feet down. It was all rocks and limbs and limbs and rocks. Once I looked up and saw a caver entangled between boulders, slithering among them as if through an intestine. Another stood atop a cliff, his six-foot frame a speck of red on the underground mountain. The experienced cavers seemed to be everywhere at once, scouring passages for safety and loose rocks before we entered, sometimes positioning their bodies to block our falls in case we lost our footing.

I slid once, along The Shelf with its slippery fall into a black abyss below. The only hint of what lay beneath was the sound of strong rushing waters. I lost traction on both feet and dangled from a rock I hugged with my arms.

"Are you OK?" The guardian caver yelled over the water. "Can you make it?"

Because of him, and the sight of my husband at the other end, I believed in that second that I could. I did. If I hadn't, I wouldn't be here to write anything at all. Surprisingly, the small tubes of space didn't make me claustrophobic. They made me feel comfortable, embraced by the earth, even though some were strangling and vertical. Once I faced six feet of sheer rock, higher than I was tall. The guardian stood in front of me and bent over, his hands on his knees, making a step of his back.

"Walk on me," he said. I hesitated. "Use me. Go ahead."

My boot found his spine. I felt his flesh move when I propelled myself up. "You're a saint," I said, my voice rising with the exertion on the last word.

Another pitch-black vertical passage was so close I could only fit in it alone. I had to find the strength to reach up and grasp the hand of one of the pros. The climber behind me verbally directed me to a foothold she could see from below. Using it gave me the leverage I needed to raise myself. I screamed as I did, though, because by that time my bruised left shin was tender and bleeding.

Eventually we reached the Heaven Room. Brown stalactites, huge icicle-shaped mineral deposits that hang from the ceilings, were everywhere. The light from our headlamps made them look like strips of bacon. Gently, a caver touched one and then another, careful not to break them. They sounded like African drums. The photographer on the excursion took a picture of me standing in a stalagmite. Five prongs, like digits, reached up from the floor, making it seem I was standing in the palm of a giant hand. I wondered later, when I saw the picture, how often I'd stood, unaware, in the hand of God.

The rocks revealed us all as we really were—strengths and vulnerabilities. The cavers talked us through a fear of heights, claustrophobia attacks and crises of confidence at the brink of cliffs. As I climbed, it occurred to me that kindness is a survival tool, and that our largest fears can be surmounted with the love and skill of those who travel with us to the dark places. The revelations came faster after that:

- We are part of the elements, not masters of them.

- There are still men who measure their prowess in discovery, not dollars. I wondered if people above ground recognized who these cavers really were.

The way out was the same as the way in—only generally more up instead of down. Twenty feet from the surface, in a straw-shaped passage, my headlamp went out. I had batteries in my backpack but no room to get at them. The caver in front of me realized my plight.

"I'm going to look down at you," he said. "When I do, memorize the rocks in front of you for a couple of feet so you can climb them. Then I'll do it again."

The metal of his helmet scraped the earth until a beam of light illuminated the muddy rocks above me. He crawled up a couple of feet and I followed. Another scrape, another fast beam, another vertical scramble. Oh, to know the earth this way, to feel my way through her, to see she is a pulsating, shifting, living thing like me. The last two feet were at hand, the caver said. His body pushed up and out and, for the first time in five hours, I saw sun. I crawled through the last tight grasp, breaking into light and heat, and laughed out loud when I stood beneath the sky again.

I'd made it and in the process understood my own sublimated need to crawl through the dark and dangerous womb of Mother Earth, just as my daughter had grown in mine. My journey 160 feet below the surface was my way of trying to experience what she did, and my way, after I realized I would not have a second biological child of my own, of restoring my faith in birth itself. I also understood an eternal impulse inside me and all of us — call it God — to risk everything for a chance to glimpse the sun.

I had re-enacted my own rebirth and in so doing created the confidence to birth whatever I could. Creations of words. Creations of hope.

10,000 flowers

Some Hindus believe we are each born with a finite number of breaths, just enough to fulfill our mission for this lifetime. One of my writing mentors, a prolific author, says she believes we are born with a finite number of words. That is why, she quips, she writes very brief emails and even keeps her grocery lists short. I found my favorite sentiment in this vein in a greeting card in a tiny shop at a zen center in the New Jersey Pinelands. "To find the Buddha, look within," it reads. "Deep inside you are ten thousand flowers."

For a flower to open takes almost no energy. To keep it from opening, though, takes a lot. Occasionally I mentally inventory which flowers are inside me now, which have seen their day and spilled their seed, which refuse to close though their season is over and, most importantly, which beg to be opened but still are not. Each plays an important role in the budding of consciousness.

The colorful storybook of my maternal ancestors already has been opened, but my paternal ancestors always were a closed-off part of my inner garden where few happy stories bloomed. In 1929, the year of the stock market crash, my dad's parents abandoned him. The way I heard the story, he and his younger sister awoke one day to find they were the only people in their Jersey City apartment. Their parents had vanished. My dad, then six, took his sister by the hand and walked out the door. The two children set out toward their grandparents' home, which they knew was somewhere in the city. They kept asking people which way to go until, eventually, they arrived.

The grandparents, Felice and Madelina, were Italian immigrants who had birthed 22 children, most of whom died young. On the 1910 U.S. Census my great-grandfather listed his profession as "Shoe polish." They were poor, these two, but they took in their two grandchildren, their namesakes, and raised them. My father adored his grandmother, who died when he was sixteen. At her wake he put his class ring in her casket. When it closed, it contained the only thing of monetary value he had ever owned. What did not close, however, was the legacy of this woman who did what she had to do to support her family. Every Thanksgiving she killed and cooked the turkey the Democratic Party gave out to its constituents. Otherwise, there would have been no holiday dinner.

Dad's mother never reappeared in his childhood. His father, Rocco—a prizefighter who went by "Rocky" professionally—did show up. I recall my dad saying Rocco called himself "Rocky Kansas." Unfortunately, Rocco used his son as a punching bag on his occasional visits. There was one incident Dad never forgot; it evoked from him a sense of integrity so strong it lasted his whole life. One day, he recounted, Rocco visited in rare form—belligerent, bossy and drunk. "Who do you love more?" he demanded. "Me or your grandmother?" Dad answered squarely, "My grandmother." Incensed, Rocco belted his son. Again, he asked. Again, the same answer. Another punch. The encounter escalated until Rocco carried my dad to the second floor of the house and held him out the window by his feet. He asked again and got the same answer. I always have envisioned that scene, Felice and Madelina yelling at their son to

stop, maybe swiping at him with a broom or whatever was nearby. Dad was brought inside, safely.
Who can blame him for not wanting to honor a
parent like that?

Alcohol, I am told, played a role in Rocco's early
demise. He died in his 40s, probably around the
time my dad entered the United States Navy in the
waning days of World War II. After the war, my
dad went to law school on the G.I. Bill of 1944. His
mother reappeared in his adult life only once — via
a phone call after she read in the newspaper that he
had graduated law school. She said, "Congratulations." He said, "No thanks to you," and that was
that. Dad's early days filled him with compassion
for the powerless and the poor. He was a champion
for them his whole life, even to the point of repre-
senting people for free, which hurt him financially.
For my dad, the law was never about profit. As he
told the young attorneys who apprenticed with
him, "You've got to learn the law is not a business.
It's a calling." This passion, combined with sheer
determination and, frankly, a brilliant mind, propelled him through a stunning career. His small
office was known as a place people could go for fair
and fiery representation.

The truth, though, is that no generation on a
family tree can be skipped. Each person on it, no
matter what they did, represents a flower in our
ancestral garden and cannot simply be yanked.
There is loss and grief in my dad's childhood story.

Both may be held in silence, but they are held. While researching various kinds of emotional healing techniques, I discovered the worldwide Family Constellations work of German psychotherapist and psychoanalyst Bert Hellinger. It puts forth the notion that familial love flows in an order that, when disrupted, impacts the generations to come. The consequences of an unresolved conflict between two people somehow will play out down the familial line between and among people who were not even born when the original difficulty erupted.

Hellinger's therapy helps families bring these patterns to consciousness by role playing, sometimes with actors taking on the role of deceased ancestors. Family Constellations fascinated me because of the stillbirth of my daughter and one-on-one work with other mothers whose infants died. Acknowledging a deceased infant in the family line, and giving that infant his or her proper place on the family tree, is necessary if the love flow in the family is to proceed normally.

A friend of mine still has a difficult relationship with her elderly mother, who was unable to come to grips with the death of her first daughter, killed in an accident at age seven. My friend, the second daughter, was constantly compared to the imagined perfection of her deceased sibling. Because of the girl whose death she never quite accepted, the mother never quite saw the unique beauty of my friend. Every person, no matter their fate, needs to have a place on the family tree, if not for the love of that soul, then for the love of the souls who follow.

The story of my dad's parents, though rarely mentioned, exuded power nonetheless. My brother and I learned we were descended from two ne'er-do-wells who gave up on the very life they created. Given the rough historical context, many forces must have been at work in the story, not the least of which was the financial desperation wrought by the Great Depression. I researched the story in an attempt to pop up a few more of the 10,000 important flowers inside me.

I started with Rocky Kansas and found he was more than a boxer. Known as "Little Hercules," Kansas was the lightweight champion of the world in 1925 and 1926, the golden era of boxing. Newspapers described him as a 5'2", 133-pound Italian bullyboy with fierce determination. He had been recruited to box at age 16 when he was a newsie on the streets of Buffalo. Not until age 30, old by boxing standards, and after three attempts to wrest the title from Benny Leonard, did Kansas—the original "Rocky" champion—finally win the world championship against Jimmy Goodrich. Kansas was dogged and disciplined, enduring 17 operations on his face and hands during his career. *The Biographical Dictionary of American Sports* reports Kansas was known for his experimental blows and had "a fighting style as formless as the prose of Gertrude Stein." An underdog who never gave up, he was a huge favorite of fans in the years after World War I and drew thousands to his fights nationwide, even at Madison Square Garden. During his career he saved $200,000, not bad for a guy who started out delivering newspapers. He lost every cent in the crash of 1929.

But not even that loss defeated him. Years later, the Buffalo papers, describing the fighter as "good-natured and philosophical," quoted him as saying, "I haven't any complaints. It was a tough life but a good one." Immediately after the big crash, he started working construction jobs to regain some of his fortune. As long as he could work with his hands, he said, he would be OK. The more I read about Kansas, the more I wondered about what had happened to him. He sounded like a hero and bore no resemblance to the bullying Rocco who hung his son out a window.

In fact, Rocky Kansas was known as a gentleman outside the ring. After he died in 1954 from cancer, his hometown Buffalo paper relayed a telling tale from his life:

> One night, on one of his infrequent visits to a friend's tavern, Rocky was standing silently at the bar sipping a soft drink when a belligerent, heavy-set fellow wandered in, promptly knocked two patrons down and started to heckle Rocky.
>
> "Go away, please," said Rocky. "Don't bother me. I'm an old man and I don't want any trouble."

But the big guy wanted trouble. When he woke up, he was outside in the cold, night air because Rocky might have been an "old man," but he was a hard-hitting "old man."

Rocky Kansas's real name, I learned, was Rocky Tozzo. So I approached my 85-year-old dad with the discrepancy, even as I handed him some stories I had unearthed about Rocky Kansas. My dad's eyes lit up.

"Wow!" he said. "Articles about Rocky Kansas! He was my hero."

Perplexed, I asked whether it was his father. He said no.

"But wasn't your father Rocky Kansas?" I inquired.

"In his dreams," Dad replied.

"But isn't that what he called himself?"

"You'll never find anything about my father in any boxing hall of fame. My father was a nobody. He'd call himself Rocky Kansas to buck himself up, like the name was a good luck charm. It didn't work." Then, enamored with the papers I had handed him, he said, "I'm going to sit down and read these. Rocky Kansas. This is great."

Turns out, I had not found my ancestor. Or had I? The real Rocky Kansas had had two sons, Vincent and Kenneth. But I think he had lots of sons in actuality. How many kids, like my dad, had he inspired? My dad, I realized, had all of Rocky Kansas's qualities—the fight, the ingenuity, the determination. Somehow, I thought, my dad had in his mind adopted Rocky Kansas as the father he never had. The two Rockys were both prizefighters, part of that early "Italian mauler" tradition, as it was known. They worked with their hands and their spirits. But in the case of my dad's father, it all went bad. True champions don't fight when they don't have to, they only choose opponents of equal or superior caliber, they understand their power (physical and inspirational) and they persevere.

In all the ways my dad's father went wrong, Rocky Kansas went right, and there was a boy in New Jersey closely watching both men as each showed him the depths and the heights to which a human being can take himself. In his heart, my dad chose Rocky Kansas as his hero and, as I pondered Dad's response to the stories about the boxing legend, I decided that I, too, would choose Rocky Kansas as a spiritual grandfather, a true ancestor in so many ways. Why not choose that? Why not choose to feel related in spirit to the man so beloved by the men he had fought that they carried his casket at his funeral? So beloved that eight priests officiated at his funeral mass? Why not? The legacy of Rocky Kansas, which so ignited my dad's imagination and admiration, lit mine, too.

In this way, another flower blossomed inside me. I do not regret finding out about these two Rockys because now I know more about the story into which I was born. In that story it must be said that my paternal grandfather lived and died. He died in body and to the divine spirit within him that could have changed him into a champion, if not in the ring then in the life of his son.

What worries many of us is not so much our deaths, but the end of our stories. We want to control our own futures, our legacies. But the story of my daughter's death, a breach with the future, and the story of my paternal grandfather, a breach with the past, have taught me not to worry about ends because there aren't any. None of us can know what we mean in the scheme of life. We live inside stories. In some we are heroes. In others we play bit roles. But our sound and fury on this earth, even when silenced, are always part of the unfolding godhead. We forever blossom, in one form or another, somewhere in the divine consciousness. Every flower is eternal in the great garden of the gods.

Choosing whom to believe

Proverbial knives still cut

If our spiritual stirrings sound more like a cacophony than a symphony, it may be because the messages we hear in the echo chambers of our minds are not our own. These potent intangibles are unseen, which is the only thing they have in common with our inner divine nature. Otherwise, they do little more than confound and mislead us. It is never too late, though, to realize the voice prodding us and the pattern of reactions we follow—all of which disrupt and upset us so—are simply not ours. Sometimes others plant within the gardens of our minds their own unrealized hopes for the future, their unlived dreams, their angst, their desperation. In our bodies these forces feel foreign, which is why we wrangle with them and, in so doing, wonder what is wrong with us.

In the Gestalt classic *Don't Push the River*, author Barry Stevens makes a distinction between the ability to think—intelligence—and actual thoughts. She posits that a sharp and well-exercised mind will create a self-concept with whatever thoughts are available to process. If we process impulses and wonderments from our soul, our self-concept will be sound. If, however, the mind is processing thoughts implanted by others, the resulting self-concept will be turbulent and never feel quite right. This disruption can find its way into even our smallest likes and dislikes. Stevens writes:

> *When I was sick and sorting myself out, one of the things I did was take the words "I don't like pink" (which I had often said) and let the words somehow pick up something from the past and see where they came from, because they certainly didn't fit me. ... I heard "a voice" in my ears, saying Idon'tlikepinkIdon'tlikepink over and over and over, rapidly. I listened. That's all, just listened. The "voice" became three voices, then clearly all three became female voices, and then they came through as my mother's voice, my sister's voice, and my Aunt Alice's voice. It doesn't matter here what I learned from that. I saw a whole configuration and "I don't like pink"*

was totally clear to me. Someone else didn't like pink.

I know what she means. I entered my journalism career after working in supplementary capacities in my father's career—law. I crossed the threshold with treasures I'd learned from working with my father: Focus so forceful and encompassing that through the years I have affectionately referred to it as "demonic." A powerful aptitude to analyze, apply logic and build arguments. A respect for accuracy down to the smallest details. A passion for life. But I also entered journalism with the hard-headed insistence on rightness built into the legal profession, at least in my experience. The goal at all times, I learned, is for the client and the case to triumph, and the strategy is to never back down and to always deflect, deride, dismiss or destroy any opposing force. Having built an argument, a good lawyer defends it with soldierly and scholarly fortitude, often creating interactions that are inherently adversarial. All these traits came naturally for Dad, but that temperament didn't fit me and I often came home from work with a splitting headache.

Even after I found a work environment that fit me in every way—a newsroom—it took a decade to change the landscape of my mind and let my God-given temperament ascend. Like my father, I naturally like to ingest lots of arguments but, while he does so for the sake of supporting one, I do so for the purpose of showing myself and my readers how they interact and, most importantly, the impact those interactions have on all our lives. This is a very different mindset and the world, lest we forget, is filtered through our mindsets.

The first step in knowing our own minds, though, is challenging any unrest we feel. Tricky business indeed because those who implant pieces of their world view inside us usually do so because they want to lovingly influence us. Though not always.

In the fall after Victoria was stillborn I felt an excruciating sharp pain in my lower right back. It was not unlike the stabbing aches of late pregnancy. But my lower back had never given me trouble at any other time of my life and my pregnancy was over. Was my body telling me I was not letting go of Victoria as well as I thought I was? Was I holding myself in unhealthy postures? Oddly, no massage or exercise alleviated the pain, and it was impeding my ability to concentrate on a daily basis. Eventually I sought out a local practitioner of Rubenfeld synergy, a system of healing created by Ilana Rubenfeld which assumes that all dimensions of our being are connected and that an emotional or spiritual wound may manifest physically. The system, which utilizes talk and touch, holds that a release of dis-ease on one level automatically will travel through all levels of our personhood. I wasn't sure what that meant but it sounded right to me because to be a stillbirth mother is to understand that one pain can permeate mind, body and heart in one fell swoop. So off I went to Margaret, a Rubenfeld synergist, who offered me tea as we chatted in comfortable chairs about my symptom and the most recent happenings of my life.

Skeptical but willing, I reclined on her table. She asked me to put my hand on the place that hurt. Leaning to one side, I did. Gently Margaret placed her hand there and spoke to me in soothing tones that lulled me into a meditative, even quasi-hypnotic, state. I found myself speaking to her from a different place than my mind. Tears rolled down my face. The answers I provided to her questions were as surprising to me as they were to her. Our conversation was very short.

"What does this pain feel like?" she asked.

"Sharp."

"What kind of sharp?"

"Like a knife. She put a knife in my back and then abandoned me. Now I'm walking around with a knife."

"Who is she?"

"My friend from college." I told Margaret about a woman who suggested to me in my tender post-birthing state that if I killed myself I could be with my daughter. As I spoke my back muscles tightened.

"Those were sharp words." Margaret said. My lower back arced in pain.

"They certainly were. She also told me she couldn't share with me anymore because I must be so jealous that she has children and my child died and I almost died trying."

"In what tone did she deliver that statement?"

"She was gleeful."

"Um-hum." Margaret lowered her face to the level of mine. My eyes being closed, I sensed the movement and heard her soft voice directly in my ear. "Let it fall out."

"What?"

"Stop holding the knife. It's not yours. Let it fall out."

Instantly, my back relaxed and I practically heard the clank of metal on the wood floor below the table. The pain stopped as quickly and easily as if someone had turned off a running faucet. Margaret told me to rest and left the room.

I was astounded and my inner circuits were flooded with the reality of what I had just learned: I can hold things that hurt me and don't belong to me and, more importantly, I can let them go. That pain, ten years in the past at this writing, has never returned. Not a twinge. To release it meant I had to let go of the offending sentiments I had been offered, certainly not in love, as well as the relationship from which they came. Of course it is a struggle to release any long-standing relationship, but release is the only option when staying attached includes self-harm.

So profound was this healing, and so fast, that it caused me a few years later to go on a kind of spiritual healing tour of America to see what other techniques existed and what they had in common. Ilana Rubenfeld is right: All dimensions of our being—body, mind, emotions and spirit—are connected. That may sound like bad news when I recall the complete agony that had kept me hostage for almost three months. The flip side, though, is that a healing intercession in any one dimension creates a ripple effect through the others. Different healing modalities enter different portals of our being in different ways but they're all about achieving total freedom from dis-ease. Perhaps one person responds well to a mental healing suggestion, as I did, but another, by her very nature, would prefer a shamanic journey or a surgical operation. Any way it happens, healing is a way to stop the old hurtful pattern and give the so-called patient a chance to establish a new and healthy one, unimpeded by pain.

Many portals opening to one road of health. To me that sounds a lot like being able to talk to many faces of God. Both have the power to reshape, change and heal us from within. Ours is a wondrous existence.

The sounds of silence

As the proverbial doctor says, though, an ounce of prevention is worth a pound of cure. After the Rubenfeld incident I became aware of what I ingested. Much of what we are offered — from punitive belief systems to fat-laden fast foods — does not nourish us. During my college years I cannot count the number of times I was offered recreational drugs — from pot brownies to acid — as if I were being handed nirvana on a platter. This is nurturance? I never succumbed and still shudder to think of the entire mind-body cascade being taken over by a recreational drug. Look at the havoc even a well-timed hateful sentence can wreak.

But such is true of all kinds of language. Enlightened words, like their hurtful, careless or ignorant counterparts, travel far and deep into the pathways of individual consciousness. For me writing well and staying well are inextricably linked.

Since the Rubenfeld healing I have been very aware, too, of thoughts that enter my mind and create a series of reactions, perhaps starting with a nebulous (or not so nebulous) emotion or a physical sensation. I like to trace these reactions backwards. Almost always the image of a tree arises in my mind's eye. A single thought is a branch on a limb leading to a trunk and down to a root. There are lots of old trees and lots of old thought patterns with long histories and well-watered roots. I've chosen to think of this process as fascinating rather than distressing and, accordingly, that's how it unfolds for me. One day recently, for instance, I was sent an email by an authority figure chiding me for some action I took in a situation about which she had no background or knowledge. I had broken a rule but had done so not to violate an even more important rule. Nonetheless the email reprimanded me and indicated no further discussion would be had on the matter, even to the extent that I was not permitted to reply to the email on my own behalf.

Intellectually, I knew the issue was small and unimportant, but after I read the message, I nonetheless felt a deep anger flare up inside me and I wanted to weep. In moments I traced the feeling down to its roots, closed the email and moved on to better things. I needn't respond to the suggestion that I should be silent in such a low-stakes situation. But the flare-up was real before it vanished. What had happened? At many pivotal times in my youth I had been told to be silent, evoking quiet emotions of despair because I felt I was being negated. Squelching those emotions now is easy for a simple reason: I understand they are attached to a message and remember I have chosen not to believe in the message. Deactivating the message stops the emotional loop. Not all messages that are sent are worthy of being received even once, never mind multiple times throughout our lives.

Let us trace this silence message in the annals of my memory.

In college I was an eager and enthusiastic student of literature. I always have loved how words weave themselves through and among thoughts and perspectives. In high school, English was the only subject in which I took advanced placement courses and, during the summers, studied on the college level. I couldn't wait to actually study at that level all the time. In one of my first courses at the university, though, I met up with an English professor with a clear message for the whole class: "Odds are you're not fit to contribute to literature. Think of Wordsworth, Coleridge, Blake, Keats, Milton and ... you. Do yourself and the rest of us a favor and don't even try. Let me help you find a reason to disqualify yourself from trying." In individual sessions in his office he personalized the message for each of us, leaving many students bewildered and discouraged and scrambling for their catalogs to see what other course of study they might take. His message made me a little dizzy at first but the spell passed. I did not understand why a professor would teach from such a starting point.

Earlier in my life I'd encountered such teachers. In high school I played guitar in a music ministry and one afternoon brought to a rehearsal in the auditorium a new arrangement I had written for a standard hymn. Intrigued, my musical friends, all seniors, started playing it when suddenly we heard a loud cracking sound. The auditorium doors had swung open and hit the wall. A nun, the musical director, bounded down the main aisle, face red, arms flailing. My heart beat wildly. What was wrong? Was there a fire? The nun stopped at our music stands and roared, "Who wrote this arrangement?"

I raised my hand.

"You!" she wailed, pointing at me. "Get into my office. Now!" I put down my guitar and followed her up the aisle, out of the auditorium and to the music room, where she shut the door, pushed me against the wall and stood an inch from my face. "Who do you think you are writing your own arrangements? Mozart? What makes you so high and mighty?"

"Sister, respectfully," I said, "I'm trying to grow my musical ability —"

"Shut up!" she yelled. All I remember her saying after that was the group would play the arrangement as she had written it. I hadn't known the original arrangement was hers. One more directive: I was never to arrange another song for the music ministry again.

Back further on the tree, another high school scenario: A visiting poet held workshops for the junior class. A real poet! I was entranced. He gave us an exercise to write, then another, and asked for volunteers to read their work. Several other girls read and I did, too. When we had finished he asked some of us to leave the room. Baffled, we looked at each other, then him, until he explained it was so clear we weren't writers we'd best spend our time in study hall in the next building and get some homework done. Mystified, I gathered my books and walked with the others into the hall. The French and forensics teacher, an elderly nun, passed us going in the other direction. She asked what we were doing in the hall since classes were in session. I told her. In disbelief she held her hands together, as if in prayer. "Good Lord deliver us," she said. "Don't worry, Sister," I replied. "It's just that he doesn't see I'm a writer." That response still amazes me. The voice of my soul must have told me not to listen to the poet.

The truth is, our culture is awash in messages of silencing. Some women in the world of my childhood and coming-of-age years routinely endured astounding experiences of abuse and belittlement, all told in hushed tones behind closed doors. The tales were shared with an audience of one or two friends, sometimes in tears, almost always with the only encouragement being the touch of another woman's hand. I thought to myself at a very young age, *What does it mean, this silence?* Whole identities were locked up in silence. So many people are never allowed to articulate the words that would help them heal or grow. After a time, it seems, their every impulse to speak or create is met with an inner tsunami of conditioning that automatically envelopes the impulse, picks it up and breaks it on the shore of consciousness. That is an important shore, an essential place of passage where the inner stirrings of confidence and creativity either drown or flow into words, images, inventions, theories and actions that we sail into the world.

To teach silence must offend the muses and certainly runs counter to the creative divine energy with which we are all born. No matter how many authority figures angrily demand or lovingly recommend our silence, there is only one force that can actually cause us to fall mute — ourselves.

A single voice of love

Led by a faith and a vague inner knowing, I persevered in writing despite all attempts to trash my creative independence, mostly because I saw no other way of being that suited me better. Writing is enormously interesting and fresh every day. The right words can change lives, beginning with the life of the writer. Literature, written or read, is sheer personal alchemy. It can spin the pain of life into the gold of healing and wisdom.

Eventually I met a special professor at Fordham University in the Bronx. Knowing my background (because he asked for it), he shared his own considerable inner struggles and vulnerabilities. What's more, he kept talking to me and showing me how he worked his way out of the troubles of his life. I took mental notes.

George, chairman of the department, found innovative ways to tell me difficult things. I was a graduate assistant in the master's program and so worked in the department offices. One day he gave me a letter to type. Headset over my ears, fingers gliding over the keys of a red electric typewriter, I learned about his alcoholism. How he fell into it. How at his lowest point he beat his wife with a garden hose. How he divorced and remarried her. How he had become a sponsor in the years since he recovered. Turned out the letter was to me. The afternoon I typed it, he did not emerge from his office until the workday had ended and the department secretary had gone home. He sat on the other side of my secretary's desk and regarded me.

"Now you know something you didn't know before." He lit a cigarillo.

"Yes."

"Any kind of transformation is possible. We choose who we become."

"I see."

"And, by the way," he said, "don't call me 'Doctor' anymore. Makes me sound like your gynecologist. You can call me George."

Some people called him Saint George, I later learned, and for twenty years, long after I graduated, I turned to George to talk through difficult times. We talked over pastrami sandwiches in restaurants on Arthur Avenue, through letters and then emails and during my occasional visits to his home in his declining years. George was tough. He challenged most thoughts and writings I shared with him, insisting time and again, "We are distinguished by our thinking, not by our emotions." He even took me to task on the topics I chose to write about and mixed no words in telling me when he thought I was wasting my brainpower. Some conversations got hot and heavy. Once he said, "I'm not asking you to agree with me. I'm asking you to think about it until you do."

"Jesus, George," I'd say. "What does that mean?"

"It's my job to condition your mind so it can filter your soul the best it can," he said. That was years after it was his job to officially teach anybody anything. "And you know why I took the job? Because I love you, that's why."

Once I asked him for a letter of recommendation for a job and he handed it to me over lunch. It said that of all the students he had ever taught, he rated me in the top one percent when it came to creative intelligence. It said he would consider any advantage or courtesy that was extended to me a personal favor. I folded the letter and put it back in the university envelope. "Now you know what I think of your talent," he said. "Here's a thought for someday when I'm not here: You would make a great professor. But judging from the way you take care of watering the plants in the office, you'd make a lousy nurse."

George was tough for the purpose of growing me, not silencing me. That man was more than a teacher. He embodied the archetype of teaching itself and to this day I still mull points he asked me to consider. I have grown around those points even after his death. His lone voice propelled me confidently down a path I otherwise may have walked tentatively. He and I met, soul to soul, and I chose to believe him. There always is a counter voice to the cacophony of negative and apathetic voices that besiege us all. If we listen for words uttered in love and respect, we will hear them. Even one will do, and that one word, if we dare believe it, will erase years of damage.

George told me I wrote best when I got personal. There came a day I started to pen the story of my daughter's stillbirth. I wrote and I wrote and, as I did, another true teacher (also a great and accomplished author) came into my sphere and edited the manuscript. "It's ready to go," she said. "Now get it out there for everyone who needs it." I sent the manuscript into the world. At the time George's health was failing and he hardly left his home. Negative responses to my manuscript started rolling in from publishers, who opted against publishing *any* story about stillbirth. I did not take their rejections personally.

Early in the life of the manuscript I brought part of it to one of the nation's most prestigious writing conferences where I had signed up for a one-on-one evaluation with a famous author. Following instructions, I had sent several pages in advance so the author could read them ahead of time and prepare for the critique. Having expended time, money and effort to attend the week-long conference, I entered the critique room, where she sat alone. I had the same enchanted feeling with which I had greeted the poet in high school and the English professor at college.

"I read your pages," said the author, handing them back to me. Her face did not bespeak pleasure. "I have two things to tell you and they're simple. First, don't write about stillbirth. Stillbirth is something that didn't happen. Write about something that happened."

I was speechless. Something that didn't happen? It sure seemed like something happened to me. A candle of understanding lit my mind. I was writing into the vast field of silence that had engulfed the stories of the women of my mother's generation, that black field that, I knew even back then, had swallowed up and invalidated the disturbing truths of their lives. Suddenly the divine spark within me leapt into flames and I knew my resolve to articulate the story of stillbirth would prevail. In the moment the flames started dancing I realized this conversation was the reason I came to the conference. Without such a response from such an erudite figure, the flame would not have grown with such necessary intensity. The famous author never would understand stillbirth because she preferred not to listen. But her preference—regarded as wisdom because of her stature—would not stop me. I remained calm.

"I'll think on that," I said. "What's the second thing?"

"Your writing is good. You'll have a book published within two years."

During my continued efforts to sell the manuscript, I introduced myself to an agent during a phone conversation set up by a mutual friend. I briefed her on the stillbirth journey described in the manuscript—one that takes the reader through the experience and tumultuous inner changes and, ultimately, into healing. When I stopped speaking there was only silence for a full minute.

Finally, the agent spoke. "You're telling me you wrote the story of your daughter's stillbirth?"

"Right."

"How nice for you, dear, but, I am quite certain, merely an indulgence of depression no one will want to read. I certainly don't."

Our mutual friend had suggested we talk because the agent, like me, had experienced a full-term stillbirth.

That night I wrote to George, who always wanted to be kept up on news. He wrote back, "Dear Lorraine, Please do not forget that the majority is always wrong. Love, George."

A publisher signed on the book, saying it illuminated a part of life important to a lot of women. *Life Touches Life* has been around the globe and back again. It has started conversations, validated thousands of grief journeys and helped widen the definition of motherhood. My readers and I have held, fascinated and freed each other. We have delivered each other into newness and courage and have become bolder and better people. The book has been excerpted in the eighth edition of a nursing textbook — the first edition to include a chapter on how to care for a mother whose baby dies. The book has been recommended to bereaved mothers by social workers and therapists throughout North America, and it has traveled to the halls of Congress to shed light on the need for funding stillbirth research and for new protocols for pregnancy monitoring in the United States. The written word here has caused a long chain of positive effect and there is no question: It all began over pastrami sandwiches in the Bronx back in the '80s.

We can choose to believe the people who leave us with psychic knives in our backs, the people who scream our insignificance into our faces, the people who ignore us and would prefer we not give voice to who we know we are in our deepest places. But beware. If we choose to believe a knife-thrower, we'll wind up stabbed. If we choose a silencer, we'll wind up voiceless.

Anybody can and will inject poison into our minds, but our souls get to decide who and what we believe. Ultimately, we know who loves us. We know who understands what each of us really is — a divine delivery system that, if encouraged to open and flourish, has a particular and important divine light to shine in this world.

Accepting supernal help

Saints actually do march in

On a brutally hot July Saturday I drove my Subaru, laden with the makings of a workshop called *The Spiritual Journey of Infant Loss*, toward Boyerstown, Pennsylvania. Green farmlands rushed by my windows as I rolled through towns that were half suburban, half rural. My head pounded and, with each mile, my nausea grew greater. I was headed to meet some dozen bereaved parents at an historic bed-and-breakfast and spend the evening with them around a table in a formal Victorian dining room. We would have the inn to ourselves. The group, organized by a *Life*

Touches Life reader, was kind enough to put me up there for the night.

I had looked forward to spending time with the group; I believe in the healing that takes place when kindred spirits share with one another from a place of respect. I believe in stopping the relentless flow of scheduled activities to make such a gathering possible. That night the dining room would serve the same purpose as the Omega woods. We would show our true colors in spite of the great whitewashing with which the culture paints over our grief. Yet the flow of my own life was particularly relentless then. The demands of working full time and caregiving and the usual list of duties that faces each of us pressed on me, so much that the week leading up to the gathering had been overscheduled. I hadn't had a chance to quiet my mind and center myself the night before, as I would have liked. Checking my watch and global positioning system, I saw I was due to meet the *Life Touches Life* reader, also a stillbirth mother, in 20 minutes. I'd make it just on time. To soothe my hot, dizzied head and queasiness I held one hand in front of the air conditioner and then rested it on my forehead. I tried to fill my mind with the words the stillbirth mother had written to me the night before: "Our 5th wedding anniversary is tomorrow and Mary Elizabeth's due date was yesterday. I've been trying to keep myself occupied by cleaning out two garages and working on your visit. What time will you be arriving? I will meet you at the inn to get you checked in. Also, I would like for the two of us to go out to eat before your presentation. We can hit Philly or King of Prussia for an early dinner."

Ugh. Food. I toyed with the idea of calling to say I was running late, giving myself extra time to pull off the road, get a cola and meditate, just to feel better. Before the idea had finished forming I realized I was tapping the side of my head to alleviate pain and pulling my car off the road to be ill. When the greens of the landscape stopped whooshing by my windows, my gaze settled on a gate and a sign. I'd stopped in front of a shrine to Padre Pio. I flashed back to my youth when I'd learned about this twentieth-century Italian Capuchin priest. I pictured him in his older years with a bushy white beard, wearing a robe, one hand raised in mid-blessing. The hand was gloved, leaving only his fingers exposed, to cover his stigmata, marks that resemble the wounds of the crucified Jesus and appear supernaturally, it is said, on the bodies of some devout Catholics. Sometimes the wounds even bleed. One day the stigmata appeared on Padre Pio after he said a mass. The saint with the kindly brown eyes was known for conducting very long masses because he would slip into deep contemplations in the middle of the services. His parishioners, taken by his holy demeanor, often sought his counsel. Then pilgrims worldwide sought him out, some saying a few minutes with Padre Pio transformed their lives.

He ate and slept very little, constantly prayed for the souls of purgatory to ascend into heaven, saw the image of Jesus in the poor and the suffering and the sick, and founded a hospital. "Bring God to all those who are sick," he said. "This will help them more than any other remedy." Padre Pio was a religious ecstatic his whole life, starting in his boyhood. He also was always sick, though doctors never seemed to know the cause of his physical problems. The saint lived with his afflictions, offering them up for the glory of God.

Padre Pio was said to possess the spiritual gifts of bilocation and miracles. He had the ability to read hearts, levitate, speak in tongues, multiply food, and see angels in bodily form. He is associated with lots of spontaneous healings the world over — before and after his death.

It had been years since I thought of the padre. I always instinctively believed in him and was drawn to the stories of religious ecstatics whose consciousness turned so inward to their divine core that they seemed to lose awareness of what was around them. Given my background, my first experiences with the phenomenon were Catholic, but in later years I recognized the same transformations in stories of Himalayan Hindu saints and Buddhist monks.

In midlife I listened, fascinated, as medical intuitive and spiritual teacher Caroline Myss spoke of how each of us vibrates with a different energy though we can be standing side by side in the same space in the same moment. She described a time she and another woman drove their car into a street riot while traveling somewhere for a spiritual purpose. As other cars were smashed or turned over, the two women rode through unscathed. Padre Pio lived that kind of life. Rarely if ever did he watch television, read newspapers or even leave the monastery in San Giovanni Rotondo. He lived on the earth bodily but his attention was in heavenly realms.

Taught from girlhood to apply the rigor of logic to all phenomena and grounded in practicality, I do not know why I instinctively loved the stories of saints like Padre Pio. Perhaps they reminded me that the world needn't be a lonely place. The very air, the saints seem to tell us, is filled with God and angels and love and, if we look closely enough, these are the realities that can fill our lungs, our hearts, our lives. But no one else in my family believed in such things. My parents were Catholic but not given in any manner to the spiritual flights of the likes of Padre Pio. I'd always felt alone in my bloodline when it came to appreciating the ecstatics.

But I had learned something new and exciting days before I went to Boyertown as I sat around a kitchen table with my parents. We were discussing an ailment for which my father was then being treated. Somehow the conversation turned toward the healing waters of Saratoga Springs, of which I had happily partaken.

"I love those waters," I said.

My mother stirred her coffee. "Not for me."

"People believe in them." I said the grandmother of a friend of mine consistently had bathed in Saratoga all her life and was now in her late nineties in good health.

"Your grandmother was the same way," my mother said. My parents exchanged a glance.

"She went to Saratoga?"

My mother put down her spoon. "To Lourdes."

My grandparents, who I called Nonna and Nonno, were both Americans but they had been born to Italian parents and spent half of every year in Italy visiting relatives. They traveled by boat. My grandmother, who suffered with chronic asthma, did not like flying. Forty-nine years into my life at the time, I didn't know she'd ever set foot in Lourdes, a town in the foothills of the Pyrenees in France where apparitions of The Virgin Mary were reported to appear to Bernadette Soubirous in the mid-nineteenth century. To this day millions of pilgrims bathe in the famous healing waters there. Apparently my proper, stately grandmother was one of them.

"Go on," I prodded my mother.

"Nonno took Nonna to Lourdes because she wanted to go. It was important to her," my mother explained. "But he never wanted to go in so he always waited for her outside, telling her to take however long she needed. She would bathe in the waters and then wear a robe as she walked to the shrine."

I could hardly picture my grandmother at Lourdes. Her faith and inclinations had been kept hidden from me. "Nonna believed in religious healing?" I asked my parents, incredulously.

"Yes." My mother tapped her coffee mug.

"So do I."

My parents looked at each other and then down, as if dejected.

"I know," they said, simultaneously.

For the first time I didn't feel alone in my intuitive appreciation for inner states in which the mind and heart do all they can to wrap themselves with the divine, to infuse themselves with it. God is many things, including medicine, as Padre Pio knew. A fragrance is said to have come from the padre's stigmata wounds, a fragrance by which many have recognized his invisible healing presence at their bedsides. Perhaps my appreciation for saints like Padre Pio helped me accept the angelhood of my daughter quickly. My Victoria Helen lives with the saints.

There on the Pennsylvania road my reverie eventually ended. I lingered in the car to say a prayer to the padre, throw him a kiss and put the car into "drive" before resuming my course. In seconds I realized I felt fine. In fact, I felt fantastic. Five minutes later I was at the inn where the still-birth mother, who had created the event, was waiting for me.

"How about we go to the Pennsylvania Dutch diner down the street?" she said. "We can walk the mile and talk." LuAnn radiated strength and love; I liked her immediately.

"Terrific," I said. "I'm famished. Let's eat." The headache did not return. The evening, which drew bereaved parents of children of all ages—and one fabulous nun—was magical.

Saints of all religious persuasions tend to walk less-traveled roads, which may be why they bring such comfort to those who find themselves on difficult life paths. People who give much and are taken for granted. People who toil for the good in anonymity and without support. People who grow sick and have no one to minister to them. People who are broadsided by tragedy and find no sufficient human companionship to comfort them. These are the people the saints visit. These are the people to whom the saints speak in the quiet of their hearts with the miraculous message, "I see you. I understand."

Jizo, the Buddhist bodhisattva of children, women and travelers, is another such saint. Pictured as a smiling old monk with a long robe and a staff, Jizo is a kind of patron saint of infants who die. No other deity I know is assigned the celestial task of ministering to these children who, according to this tradition, are sent to the Underworld after death as punishment for making their parents so unhappy. There they are made to pile up stones, which are promptly knocked down, requiring them to start over again. Jizo is said to walk through the Underworld, hide the children under his robe and scurry them out. He is a hero in the heart of every stillbirth mother I have ever known, no matter their spiritual background.

The sorrowlands

Even those of us who are not saints can help the likes of Jizo do their work. As babies who die are suddenly displaced from the warm security of their parents, so too their parents find themselves tossed inside the terrible gates of the land of infant loss. That place is bitter. There is no protection there from the elements, outer or inner. Newly bereaved parents are stunned to find themselves standing in this stark sorrowland with their arms empty, their hearts bleeding, their strength gone.

There is a corresponding sorrowland for every kind of grief and loss in the world. Whoever survives deep sadnesses is qualified to stand at the gates of these sorrowlands and walk for a time with those who newly enter. We needn't be counselors with master's degrees, saints with stigmatas, or believers in any one religious tradition. We stand as people who feel the same kind of pain, and we are inspirational simply by virtue of standing and being present.

Those of us who take on this role hear a list of oft-repeated discouragements from the larger culture. We are told that to linger in a place of pain is unhealthy for us, that we must move on to some other gate at some other passage. We are told we are indulging our depression, nursing our wounds. We are told we remain because we need the company of misery. But those who would discourage us have not known our depth of sorrow. Anyone who stands the watch understands its timeless value. If ever we touch the supernal realm, it is at these gates.

In Spring 2007 I flew to the Midwest to teach a writing-to-heal workshop at a conference for bereaved mothers. I have learned that sometimes a whole conference is worth the effort to meet even one person at the proverbial gates. Such was true in Minnesota. After my first workshop I joined my husband on the lower level of the hotel where he was manning the table at which *Life Touches Life* was being sold. Soon a gorgeous young woman walked down the stairs, stopping at each table, saying nothing, eyes wide, taking it all in. She lingered by the stacks of my book. Our gazes met.

"I'm so sorry," I said. "Do you want to talk about what happened?" She did. Briefly. She purchased a book and I did not encounter her again at the conference. Three months later, she wrote to me that I had forever left an impression on her, partly because of the book but more because I'd hugged her in a way that welcomed her to a club about which she knew nothing and which she wished she had not joined.

A good deed or word may not heal in itself but it invokes the spirits to work with us — the person doing the helping and the person helped — until we both are in some place beyond the sorrowlands, a timeless place where the dead and the living meet and the breath of God infuses the whole scenario with life and meaning. No one can claim credit for that miracle but we as individuals can set into motion the forces that converge to create it. We do this by puncturing a hole in the present and taking an action, even the smallest of actions, in love. Then the saints and the angels are summoned.

In my travels I came to learn how *Life Touches Life* helps people process the horror of many kinds of experiences. Its words invoke the spirit of Victoria, which rains down all manner of heavenly healing into the hearts of the readers. I stand in awe of this process. In letters I have received for years people write that, since they read the book, Victoria

Helen has been with them, helping them, whispering to them in the difficult nights, wiping the tears from their eyes when they struggle with feelings of defeat. She alights in their consciousness.

Victoria, a perfectly formed beautiful girl with delicate features, was stillborn on June 2, 1999, never having drawn a single breath. Yet every year on her birthday she receives cards, emails, letters and flowers marking her exquisite existence. *She receives letters of thanks and people have religious services of all kinds said in her honor. So, tell me, is she dead or alive? Is there any line of demarcation between this earthly world of flesh and pain and the divine world of faith, hope and love?*

Mike, a disabled Vietnam veteran, wrote to me after reading Victoria's story, starting a four-year correspondence that lasted until his death. In the exchange I witnessed how he chose to interact with the spirit world in a way that helped him soar when he could hardly walk. Before Mike was drafted in 1965 at age 20, he drove "a nice little car," dated a girl he knew since he was 14 and worked in his parents' printing business. In basic training for the U.S. Army he surprised himself by excelling. He was a good soldier, he said. Having grown up in the mountains of Southern California, he knew how to hide in the jungle. "I could camouflage myself," he said. "People could walk over the top of me and never know I was there."

But he could not hide from the situations in which he found himself, such as retrieving bodies after an ambush and shooting a Vietcong who, he later discovered, was a pregnant woman. After a tree fell on his back, he sustained a spinal injury. Back home he drank and acted out, harbored weapons and was jailed for a time. Flashbacks and nightmares haunted him.

Though Mike died in his early 60s, his life felt interminably long to him. Over the course of forty years the spinal injury worsened. At different times he required a bone fusion, a steel brace and an implanted electronic device, along with pain medicines. At one point Mike formed a group to help veterans in the mountain communities of Southern California collect the benefits to which they were entitled. He found some peace in that effort, but never got over feeling he and thousands of his buddies, living and dead, were neglected or forgotten.

Not until 1985 did Mike find spiritual balm for his emotional wounds. That year drug addicts living in his neighborhood harbored and abused two geese. Unable to stand the beatings, Mike waited until the end of the month, when he knew the tormentors would be short on drug money, and offered them $35 for the birds. He nurtured them back to health. Soon people from the community brought him more birds. The stream was so steady that Mike became known as "The Bird Man of

Alpine." He nursed sparrows, mockingbirds, pigeons, doves, chickens, ducks, geese, parakeets, cockatiels, lovebirds, every last one of them hurt and unwanted. "People didn't want Nam vets, either," he told me, "so I had a way of looking in the birds' eyes and seeing inside their souls."

At the peak of Mike's efforts his master bedroom served as a 30-patient nursery. He kept birds warm on a heating pad and learned how to best revive and feed them. His last rooster, which had cancer, routinely slept inside overnight in a dog carrier. In the morning Mike let him outside. One day the rooster struggled outside and Mike, sensing the end, held him until he died. But nothing made Mike's soul sing more than watching one of his feathery charges fly away and get a chance to live again.

"When I think about the buddies I lost in the war, and the family members who have passed on, I just keep hanging onto the fact they aren't really gone," he said. "You have to be aware of what's around you. They show you signs they're still here. I ask God to show me a sign and for the sight to see the sign. When I sit out back and I look at the mountains, a bird will sit and be with me awhile, and I know that's a sign. For now, that's how they come to me. It's hard to comprehend what it would be like to be free of pain and sorrow, but I still believe there is such a place and that some day I will see the guys I knew in Vietnam and we will be together again."

There are millions of ways to touch the spirit that pervades all life—as many ways as there are people. For some, like Mike, redemption is found in the cyclical mysteries of nature. One bereaved mother I know swears she is greeted by her daughter every spring in the form of the first flower to bloom in her garden. It is purple, her daughter's favorite color. The mother has an inner knowing it is a "hello" from the spirit world. Like Mike said, "They show you signs they're still here."

Snake fingers

Spirits do not permeate those places in our minds from which we make proclamations and in which we absolutely know a thing to be true, a shaman once told me. Spirits only can permeate our consciousness through doubts and questions— two states of mind that often are undervalued and, in some circles, even cause for punishment. As a person who makes her living asking questions of people in all fields from chemistry to theater, I appreciate the value of a well-framed inquiry and have found many an answer to a spiritual question in the religious texts handed down through the generations—the Sutras, the Vedas, the *Bible*, the *Koran*, the mystic psychology of *The Kybalion*. No answer comes quite as personally or with such exquisite metaphor, though, as those received on a shamanic journey accompanied by the drumming and verbal guidance of a qualified shamanic practitioner.

A journey, as a shamanic adventure is called, is a one-on-one conversation with God within the confines of the human psyche spoken in a language of imagery and references specific to the questioner. My shamanic journey may make no sense to others, nor theirs to me, and that is fine. The idea is for the individual to mull the characters, terrain, symbols and message of his journey for himself. Often a journey is like an archaeological site: it has layers of meaning.

On one such journey, led by a practitioner trained through the Foundation for Shamanic Studies, I propounded a classic midlife question about whether the long road I had traveled had delivered me to the place I was meant to be. I asked, *Have I done enough? Where should I go now and how should I get there?* Shamanistically speaking, the world is divided into the upper world (of teachers), the middle world (of physical reality) and the lower world, where my journey took place. In the lower world a journeyer encounters so-called power animals, which are associated with attributes the journeyer may need or like to possess. The animal becomes a companion for the journey.

Mine began with my Essence Self, who did not look like me. She appeared as a kind of alter ego — a woman with a tall lithe body and long black hair in a sunny meadow. Arms outstretched, she danced to the beat of the drumming though I knew intuitively it also was the rhythm of my own heart.

Essence, as I'll call her, danced in a forest clearing and descended to the lower world through a tunnel in the rocks. Upon emerging in another lush forest, she continued dancing but did not cover any ground. She was dancing in place when a huge snake appeared. It danced with her, slithering over her torso and around her head and arms. Theirs were two bodies dancing as one.

The snake said, "I move when you stand in one place. I am movement in stillness." A brown bear walked up to Essence and the snake disengaged, heading straight down a forest path, shedding skin as it went. Then I, appearing as I do in real life, emerged from Essence. The bear immediately hugged me and I watched as one small snake appeared on each of Essence's hands. They slithered around her fingers. Another unspoken message arrived: *Transformation will happen when you move only your fingers.* I understood the message: Write. All the movement I need is in my hands.

The pounding of the shaman's drum in the room in which I lay increased in rhythm and volume, the shift signaling the return of the mind to the here and now. Swiftly I leapt into Essence, who flew up the tunnel and to the woods again. Thanking her, I took my leave, opening my eyes in the room where the drumbeat suddenly had stopped. I had not expected a snake, a classic metaphor for transformation because of how it molts to renew itself. But when I thought about it — and thinking has nothing to do with the shamanic experience, which is a soul journey — I liked having met a snake.

First, the image of a snake wrapping itself around my pen instantly conjured a caduceus. That we can write ourselves into new understandings of who we are — and to even create who we become — was not a new idea for me. But the imagery was exquisitely satisfying.

Second, I interpreted the appearance of the snake in the forest to mean my soul was freed enough to explore a new way to work with the old story of the serpent in the Garden of Eden. It seemed the snake in that original story, the way I had learned it, was then imparting to me other realities about life and redemption.

While personal spiritual shifts are energetically perceptible to those who know us, they generally are not otherwise apparent. When I returned to the writing of this project, I did so with a serene confidence. A large writing project I undertook before this one involved flying and driving thousands of miles to gather information. It was exhausting in the gathering, the processing and in all ways. That movement may have expanded my breadth — valuable indeed—but not my depth, which was what the shamanic journey suggested I expand.

That night I contentedly fell into bed. The next morning I went to my computer and called up my email program, which downloaded a couple dozen messages, the last one being, SILVER SNAKE JEWELRY. I clicked on it and up came the words, "Ever notice how things run in cycles? It's time for snakes again." It contained a link to pages upon pages of an online catalog of snake rings and pendants, most of them in the swirling, circular, slithering movements of my journey. That day the middle and lower worlds seemed connected. There is nothing like inviting supernal help into our lives.

I know that for some it takes a leap of faith to participate in such a journey, particularly those of us who grew up steeped in a traditional religion, and it's even tougher for those who may have grown up in agnostic or atheist households. Ultimately, though, with no leaps, life can become too small. When we live only inside what we know and understand, the spirits cannot enter. Albert Einstein once said a problem is not solved by the same level of thought that created it. The same is true of our understanding of ourselves. We are restricted not by our beliefs but by our unwillingness to challenge them.

It has been said that the shamans of old proceeded as they did because they had no sophisticated pharmaceuticals to administer or lab reports to run. Yes, they lacked what we have but perhaps, too, we lack what they had. The rise of integrative medicine in the United States may be an attempt to infuse our sophisticated treatment facilities and protocols with the shaman's breath and vision. My asthmatic grandmother had occasion to be in many a hospital and see many a doctor. So what was she seeking at Lourdes? Padre Pio said, "Bring God to all those who are sick." What did he know? I discovered on my own trip back from the brink of death that our very cells respond to the power of God within us—a power that regenerates the will, the mind, the heart.

When we have a real-life problem like a disease or debt or depression, taking a shamanic journey may seem like the last and most impractical, irrelevant, primitive thing to do. It would be, too, if everything in the physical world wasn't put into motion by the world of spirit.

Beauty and the self

When fragments wander

S ometimes we can become so involved with one aspect of ourselves, positive or negative, that it takes on a life of its own. I'm not talking about big scary moments but a subtle shift in perception that at first only we may notice. Then that shift grows like a crack in glacial ice. A fissure may develop as we isolate an aspect of ourselves — a perceived inadequacy, unresolved inner conflict, overconfidence, unacknowledged emotion or un-lived impulse. Perhaps this vulnerable aspect — and who does not have vulnerabilities? — meets an ex-ternal drama that offers it a life of its own. If we choose the drama, the ice breaks completely and off goes that inner conflict or that unacknowledged emotion, unsupported, like a floe in Arctic waters.

I came face to face with such a split in my thirties when I was writing about a psychic healer. One Saturday I showed up early at his spiritual center, which included workshop and retail space, to observe a gathering he would lead in the afternoon. The aroma of burning sage and sweetgrass wafted in the air. New Age music played softly on the sound system. The man, who was fifty-something, had to step out and left me in the company of his shy girlfriend, who was in her early twenties. A winter sun blazed through the storefront window, shining on ceremonial pipes, drums and books in a dusty display case. As I sat and read, the girlfriend regarded herself in a full-length mirror . She turned to me and said, "I didn't know I was Nefertiti until I met him."

I looked up from my book. "Excuse me."

She ran her fingers over her pale face, her gaze never leaving the mirror. "He has powers to see past lives. Now I can see it, too. Especially if I put my hair like this." Pulling her hair back tautly from her face, she jutted out her jaw to match the regal look depicted in portraits of the wife of the Pharaoh Akhenaton of the Eighteenth Dynasty of Egypt. Akhenaton had revolutionized religion in his kingdom by declaring there was only one god, not many. The one true god, he said, was the sun, which he worshipped. According to some accounts, the pharaoh took the roofs off all his temples, the better to let in the sunshine. Like the pharaoh's queen, the girlfriend, a high school graduate who had forsaken college to assist and study with the psychic, had a long, graceful neck.

The scene took my breath away, particularly since the psychic had confided in me his belief that he was the reincarnation of Akhenaton. He even wore a sun pendant. Apparently the man lived inside this fantasy to the extent that he partnered with a woman who was not free, within the confines of the relationship, to find her own beauty. Rather she played the part of the consort to complete his drama. Lost like Shakespeare's Ophelia, the girlfriend abdicated her own inner radiance and complexity and allowed a needy fragment of herself to walk into a one-dimensional role in someone else's delusion.

Their story ended eerily. The historical Akhenaton suffered with Marfan's syndrome, the condition that afflicted Abraham Lincoln. Among the symptoms of this disfiguring disease is poor eyesight, which might help explain the pharaoh's obsession with sunlight as well as his early death. Both the pharaoh and the psychic, who also had a distinctive appearance, died at age 54. I never knew what became of the young woman, though I hope she found a way to validate her own beauty.

Any woman who has tried existing like Botticelli's Venus—a creature of perpetual youth and unchanging beauty standing in a beautiful seashell—understands the dangers of this pedestal phenomenon. When a woman gives over her effervescence to any force outside herself, she is admired, approved of and depended upon because she does not move from the place she stands. Others know where to find her when their own energy is lacking and they want to draw from the well of her life essence. But if such a Venus should so much as turn her head and look backward to the horizon above the Botticellian sea, someone would feel betrayed. If she decides to cut her flowing blonde locks, gracefully or ungracefully reference her aging, or in any way step off the pedestal and into the watery currents of her own development, she becomes unpredictable or, worse to those who would claim her, unavailable. The price for her freedom is loss of their approval and support. The reward, though, is the rein to be the morphing marvel of a woman she was born to be.

Her real beauty resides in the evolution that leads her from one version of herself to the next. It is in the sum total of who she is. Filmmaker Ken Burns once said that meaning accrues in duration. So, too, does our beauty. The beauty of a woman—or a man—does not flourish at one age or in one role and then wither. Rather, it matures through self-growth, self-compassion and self-appreciation at every phase of the life cycle. A key to getting the process back on track is in fully occupying every phase, every moment, a theme spiritual teacher Eckhart Tolle explores in *The Power of Now*.

Though we may be physically present now, Tolle writes, our mind may be elsewhere in what he calls psychological time. It may be playing a past or anticipated drama or following a line of thought about who the self should be or could have been. It is impossible to liberate the true self, the divine self, the original self — all terms are accurate — with such thoughts. Indeed the divine self requires no thinking to know who it is. Its knowing comes from the soul.

Our feelings of discontent, then, are exacerbated when the mind mercilessly "de-liberates" (to use a term from Gestalt author Barry Stevens), keeps making noise and disconnects us from the divine stillness within, the very stillness in which we mature. We live in an age, though, where the depth that comes with stillness is seen as unproductive — even undesirable — because it appears to go nowhere. In a world where speed is king and everyone is supposed to be on their way to somewhere grand, only movement gives a sense of advancement. Computers offer an individual the illusion of being around the globe in one day. We can text a friend in the next state, write an email to a potential business partner in Japan and check the stocks in Great Britain. Why not? Our technologies assure us we can miss nothing and be everywhere. Except here.

The fullness of the self

One to three years after Victoria Helen's still-birth, when it was clear I would not conceive another child, I became preoccupied with the question of whether I should become a mother anyway. In retrospect, I can see the question arose in me, framed as it was, because others asked me, "Will you become a mother?" or "Will you finish what you started and adopt?" I replied, "I don't know." To adopt or not to adopt? I searched out others' stories of adoption and how their arrangements had worked out. But no matter what they said, I didn't come closer to an answer. The question kept floating in my mind like tumbleweed, disrupting my inner peace, until finally I visited an ashram to talk to a swami. When I told him about Victoria Helen, his face screwed up in pain. "Oh, that's rough," he said. When I articulated the question that plagued me, his face brightened. "Oh, that's easy."

"Easy?"

He reminded me of a lesson I once had heard him present about the atma, the "I" self that is our ultimate identity as opposed to the smaller personality-bound "me" self. Questions are mind-numbing conundrums for "me," with its penchant for gathering information and endless thinking, are a piece of cake for "I." He bid me to present the question to the atma. No searching is required, he said. No thinking, either. Atma just knows. I closed my eyes and inwardly asked the question: *Should I be a mother?* An answer instantly surfaced: *Invalid question. You ARE a mother.* I had forgotten that atma resides at the core of myself. My answer came when I "re-membered" (to use a term from author Maureen Murdock). In spiritual terms I think of it this way: "Me" comes up with a question from its life circumstances and asks it of the divine "I," my soul. Then question and answer, moving toward each other from different directions, interlock like two puzzle pieces. The function of the mind is to form the right question; the function of faith is to let go of it.

Swami Dayananda, the guru of the swami I visited, wrote a tract called *The Fundamental Problem,* which I bought at the ashram during my visit and keep in my library. From time to time I take it off the bookshelf to remind myself the core problem of human existence is forgetting the atma is embedded in the self and the core desire of the human heart is experiencing the fullness of the self. Swami Dayananda writes:

> ...*this urge to be full, complete ... is, in fact, the desire, behind all topical desires, the fundamental desire, the mother desire, for it is the*

desire which gives birth to all desires and motivations.

So when we get the car we covet we momentarily feel good. Not because we have the car but because at the moment we get it our mind stops whirring with discontentment that we are incomplete because we don't have it. Ultimately what we want is the calmness of mind that comes when we remember we need not desire anything to be full. We are full by virtue of who we are—atma and all. (On the same theme, spiritual teacher and author Rick Jarow says abundance is "the deep realization you have everything you need to be you.")

When my atma helped me remember I already am a mother, my role became clear: I need to be the kind of mother I am and, in so doing, inevitably help validate the motherhood of every woman like me. What I truly sought was my best self, an idea that was wrapped up with conventional motherhood. I learned I could only achieve that goal by accepting myself as I am and proceeding from there.

At first we all look in unlikely places for our best selves. An all too common place to look is the bottle, as addictions counselor Roget Lockard discussed in a talk he presented with the lovely title, *Addiction: An Honest Mistake*. Lockard writes that an alcoholic believes the lie that alcohol will bring out his best self. Think of the entities speaking in that conversation—the alcoholic and his nemesis, the alcohol. When we have a relationship with an obsession, we direct our inner inquiries to it and all it ever does is reference our so-called inadequacies.

Self: I just want to feel more relaxed. Then I can do what I need to do. Otherwise, life's too difficult.

Obsession: You know you're better with me. Just a few drinks and you'll have all the courage you need.

Speaking to an obsession, or any part of our identity that has strayed, is a terrific way to continue despair. Our conversations need to expand to include the God within.

Lockard also writes that to drink alcohol is a search for control. We believe the drink will put us in control of our life. The paradox, though, is that sobriety exists not when we gain control but when a control-based approach to life is abandoned. Or, I would say, when "me" abdicates to "I." There is no control in life. There is only God, large enough to contain all problems and all solutions. As Sufi author and educator Kabir Helminski writes, "In Sufism it is taught there is a sobriety that contains drunkenness."

Let's put it plainly: We put enormous effort into fragmentation, searching for our most attractive, thin, rich, youthful, innocent, sophisticated, successful, nurturing, fertile selves. But our best self is the one that integrates all our aspects, including the weakest and poorest. When I left the hospital after delivering my daughter, I felt defeated. After some ten days of fever, ileus and trauma, I was glad to be leaving even though the unknown cause of my infection kept spiking my temperature. Still not sure I would live, I sat in a wheelchair in the hospital lobby watching people come and go through a revolving doorway and waiting for my husband to pull the car around to the entrance. Another mother from the maternity floor was wheeled next to me, babe in arms, "congratulations" balloons strung to the sides of her chair. She cheerily asked where my baby was. "The baby's dead," I said.

I was not my most triumphant self then, but the scales of innocence and sentimentality certainly had been washed from my eyes. My days in the hospital taught me only a heart that has known genuine fear can open in complete compassion. They taught me the wisest state of mind is humility because none of us can ever fathom even the next sentence in the story of our lives. The woman I was that day made possible the writer I have become. Without the heartbroken mother, the writer would not have the fabric of experience or fortitude of spirit to write her way into the world of spiritual identity.

There are paradoxes only the divine can help us embrace: there is no strength without weakness, no joy without despair, no understanding without confusion. The one force capable of holding and helping us make meaning through all the vicissitudes of life is God, the divine artist whose hand paints in our minds the imagery of our dreams and meditations — the very imagery through which we can glimpse perspectives from the heavens.

Such imagery arrived for me one day at a time I was caring for my elderly father. That morning I had been holding his hand as we crossed a street to get from a doctor's office back to my car. I made sure he didn't stumble on curbs since he seemed inattentive to traffic. He was charmed by a small boy who held his mother's hand as he crossed in the other direction and then by the sight of a nearby restaurant where a friend had taken him for a hamburger some five years earlier. Later that day, at my home, I stood before a collage of pictures of Dad as a young man — standing at attention in the Navy; smiling at his sister as she pinned a chrysanthemum on his lapel on his wedding day; cutting the cake at the reception; wearing cap and gown, one arm around my mother's shoulders, as she proudly clutched his law degree.

He had lived so many selves in one lifetime, and he and I had had so many relationships. When I closed my eyes the following sequence emerged. It is dusk on a beach lit in tones of black, white and gray. I sit alone on the sand at the shoreline, gathering my knees to my chest. A breeze blows through my hair and ripples the water's surface. The sound of the tide soothes me. Then an old man, my father, is sitting next to me and he looks into the eternal horizon, as absorbed in the sight of it as I am in the sight of him. Suddenly, all rendered in light, are many forms of my father. On the beach I see a young man, ever smiling, black hair slicked back, freshly shaven, wearing pants and a newly laundered white undershirt and holding his baby daughter in his arms. He looks over the sea as if he will sail it to places where he will do unimaginably wonderful things, and his daughter will, too. In other living sculptures of light he teaches the daughter to swim in a pool, banishes her angrily from a room for suggesting it's all right to have friends who smoke pot even though she doesn't, and instructs her in the art of negotiation as she sits beside him in a boardroom around a table where powerful men talk money and real estate.

So many thoughts and emotions blossom in me. There on the beach they fly from my forehead and my chest, each emerging as a being of light. In that instant all the light bodies, floating free, move lightly and gracefully through the air. Positioned on the brink of eternity, I understand this totality as life itself. It is all the Lorraines that are and have been and could be and all the Dads, and everyone, each adding to the splendor.

In that moment a new understanding of faith enveloped me — a faith in this ultimate context. The late Irish poet and philosopher John O'Donohue, who passed into the horizon in January 2008 at age fifty-two, put it this way: "The ultimate passion of the cosmos is the creativity of divine beauty. See, beauty is the deepest embrace of all. It's the invisible embrace in which everything that is — and even everything that is not, everything that was and that will be — are all held together."

Yet instead of holding the sustained conversations with God that reveal this beauty, we have created a culture that seems to take every available train out of the station of our own hearts. We even lay new tracks every day. Publicly our political discourse, which sets our social policies and laws, allows discussion of religious themes and questions either in culturally conservative terms or not at all. The ubiquitous world of marketing, with a financial stake in focusing on the flaws of our fragmented selves, sells us ways to perfect them. Since they are not perfectible by definition, infinite sales are guaranteed. Privately, we seek escape and relief before redemption, understandable in a social order that seems devoted to confusion. Instead of the substantively luxurious images that arise within us, we grasp cheap commercial imitations. Instead of the natural beauty we are promised by growing into our divine nature, we work at artificial beauty.

In praise of endurance

I once met a young woman with a face and skin so flawless, and a shape so voluptuous, she could have been rendered in alabaster and deemed a goddess. Despite her classic beauty, she was discontent with her appearance, criticizing her forehead, the turn of her nose and the philtrum above her upper lip. She wanted plastic surgery at age thirty.

Yet our faces reflect our identities. Jean Haner, author of *The Wisdom of Your Face*, looks at faces through the lens of Chinese face reading. She reads road maps of experience in lines and features. A bump on the rim of an ear corresponds to a strong reaction to a significant childhood event. Where the bump appears reveals the age at which the event occurred. Eyebrows reveal the level of a person's self-confidence. A horizontal line on a chin can represent a break with the past. There are lines of stress and lines of joy. Moles and birth marks show extra energy or added personal ingenuity or talent. Cheeks contain messages about willpower. Long lines that extend downward from either side of the nose and frame either side of the mouth are purpose lines.

"You'd better hope to have those lines by the time you're 50," Haner said. "If they appear, they're telling you you're doing what you came into the world to do." People who have plastic surgery to fill in their purpose lines, she said, tend to feel adrift in life. What personal forces of evolution would the woman with the classic good looks be resisting by changing her face?

A woman is never more lovely than on her wedding day, Haner said, because her face radiates with the love she feels. If that love, seasoned by trials and disappointments, radiates even decades later, isn't the glow all the more beautiful by virtue of its endurance? And aren't wrinkles marvelous evidence of cumulated experience and wisdom?

Chinese medicine holds that the macrocosm of our lives — the divine patterns alive within us — are apparent in the microcosm. Our cells, our faces, our hands, our words, our deeds all speak who we are. As I regard my fifty-year-old face in the mirror I do not lament where smoothness has given way to wrinkles but rather follow the contours of the latter. The lines reveal too much tension when it comes to working, a typical Western trait. They tell me I have lived through much sorrow and much laughter. They tell me I am fulfilling my purpose on Earth. I do not yet have enough wrinkles but I am working on that, and I will keep reading my face. It is not a record I care to erase.

A life of value

Shedding grandeur

Since my father grew up destitute he especially enjoyed taking his young family on summer vacations to exotic destinations. On one such trip I accompanied him to the clubhouse at an exclusive golf resort. My 10-year-old self stood at the sign-in counter between my father and another guest who also wanted to play eighteen holes. I looked up at the other guest as he verbally belittled the college student working the desk. Always sensitive to language, I smarted at the unwarranted dressing down. The golfer asked the student if he realized what the word "Doctor" meant in front of a name. The student reddened in embarrassment and stammered when my father, in his lawyerly way, interjected, "Isn't that something? I work in a hospital, too." The comment, wedged between the bad feelings on either side of the conversation, stopped it cold.

The doctor eyed my father warily. "Oh, yeah? What do you do?"

My father looked over the top of his eyeglasses. "I change the bedpans. Takes lots of people to run a hospital, doesn't it?" Then it was the doctor's turn to redden—in anger. The student's nervous gaze moved from one professional to the other as they glared at each other.

All my life I've encountered situations such as that one. The party hostess who notes the brand name of my coat before hanging it in the closet. The socialite I call for an interview who informs me she has "people" who make her appointments with the press. The millionaire who asks me if I can name the Newport mansion whose ceiling is reproduced in his living room.

Elitism appears everywhere there are people, including the world of the spiritually inclined. I once arrived at a home at a predesignated time to interview a man known for his ability to psychically read people. As I stood in his entry foyer, he regarded me with sad eyes and a disapproving shake of the head. "You will forgive me," he said, "but I am disappointed. I was hoping you were more evolved." Not willing to so easily give him the upper hand, I smiled and replied, "Likewise."

The dynamic is always circular. A person sets a standard of alleged and usually false superiority and then judges — or pities — others for not meeting it. If it were not for the sad reality that many people fall into the trap, and start judging themselves by the snobbish and arbitrary standards of others, the maneuvers would be amusing.

Much of this manipulating passes for the trappings of success, presented as a place or state which a person occupies or does not occupy. This posturing is ridiculous and, even more, a waste of time and personhood. Success has nothing to do with grandeur or cumulation or living in what Henry David Thoreau once called "a larger and more luxurious box." Success is not excess and should not be confused with superfluous wealth which, as my favorite Transcendalist also said, buys only superfluities. Success is not about conducting business well or doing business at all. That's livelihood, though a business can be both successful and lucrative. Success is not being photographed at the most expensive places. That's publicity. Likewise, success is not having an endless to-do list. That's busyness.

There is nothing the matter with grandeur or cumulation, superfluity, publicity or busyness or even living on an estate the size of the palace of Versailles. A person may be wealthy and successful but he is not the latter because he is the former, and the same is true of poverty. Success is discovering our inner value and living it. It is a small, deep and private affair between each of us and God.

House outside, house inside

I take us now on another shamanic journey to the upper world, the world of teachers. This type of meditation, as explained in chapter five, helps an individual tap inner wisdom through imagery and story. Reclining on the floor and listening to a drum, I ascended into my metaphoric world on the back of a condor, a bird considered sacred in some circles. My intent was to ask a spirit teacher what my success looked like.

The sensation of flying was exhilarating — the rhythmic movement of the mighty wings, the cool air of the azure sky, the brilliance of the sunlight. In little time I approached the Mount of Teachers. When I alighted from the condor, I went to the main gate where Socrates sat. He said to mingle with the sages. So I walked past the gate and into crowded streets of stone and dirt. The place was busy as a market. Everywhere I looked were sages attired in styles apropos to the era and geography of their human lives. Some dress was aboriginal and Native American. Ancient prophets wore togas and sandals, the eighteenth-century philosophers the leggings and breeches of their day, and so on.

They paced in pairs or small groups, conversing as they walked past storefronts and dwellings, each of which featured not a kind of ware but a certain thought. There were houses of mythology, philosophy, psychology, theology and poetry as well as theaters where groups gathered to dramatize how different ways of thinking play out in human scenarios.

My attention was drawn beyond the town to a green mountainside where more sages sat on grass in the sun. Below them a sea as sparkling as the Mediterranean rolled out. Condors soared overhead. On I walked until I was in the midst of the wise ones and then beyond them at the edge of a wood where I encountered an old Chinese man reminiscent of Lao Tzu. Tufts of white hair sprang from his head. His white beard reached his stomach. When he smiled he showed yellowed teeth and his brown eyes shone brightly. I slipped my hand in his and we walked into the wood to a clearing where a tiny one-room structure stood. It had a chimney and a window in front and back. Inside was only enough room for the ancient and me to sit at a wood table on two simple chairs. He entered and motioned for me to join him.

"Is this where you live?"

He shook his head. "This is the house of your success."

I took in the tiny food preparation counter behind him and the sliver of a bed against one wall. "Why so small?"

The ancient lifted one hand, then one well-wrinkled finger. "Success is one tiny significant thing."

"What thing?"

"The thing that lightens your heart," he said.

"But it can take years to find that thing. It's a complicated journey."

"Success is a moment of understanding." He pointed to his head. "All the years of doings are actings on that understanding."

The shaman's drum beat more rapidly, signaling the end of the journey. I thanked the ancient and ran out the door of my success, across the green mountainside, through the town and to the gate and, having found the condor, leapt on his back and flew over the Mount of Teachers, through the skies of possibility and back to the journeying room where I lay snug with a yoga mat below me and a blanket over me. The house, with its aroma of freshly cut wood and sea air blowing through the open door, refocused my mind away from familiar patterns of thought about success and scale.

Since the house of success seemed about the size of Thoreau's cabin, I visited again that great literary ancestor from the mid-nineteenth century in the pages of *Walden* where he wrote of traveling on inner private seas—"the Atlantic and Pacific Ocean of one's being alone" — and urged each reader to "be a Columbus to whole new continents and worlds within you." Different era, different tradition, same idea.

Thoreau wrote his masterpiece about the two years he lived in a cabin ten feet wide and fifteen feet long on Walden Pond whose depth he once measured at 107 feet. He built the cabin, preferring to live away from the town of Concord. He was no conformist when it came to lodging, eschewing even curtains and preferring instead to let the sun and moon peek into his humble abode. When a lady offered him a mat, he reflected on the gift and declined, saying he would prefer to wipe his feet on the sod in front of his door than waste his time shaking out a mat. He would rather sit on a pumpkin, all to himself, than on the velvet cushions of a crowded train. So thoroughly did he resent needlessly expending precious life energy on what he considered non-essential niceties that he once wrote:

> *I had three pieces of limestone on my desk, but I was terrified to find that they required to be dusted daily, when the furniture of my mind was all undusted still, and I threw them out the window in disgust.*

If I'd taken the time to look, I would have found Thoreau on the Mount of Teachers. But perhaps he'd gone fishing, as he was wont to do. His writings caused me to ponder my own actual home —

the two thousand-square-foot brick-and-mortar place I live with my husband. It is so small and unadorned as to not register on the Richter scale of conventional success. Built in 1901 when my street was a bungalow community for a man-made lake a quarter-mile away, my home is a product of its time and purpose. It has three floors, counting the attic. The second floor contains a bathroom, a walk-in closet and three small bedrooms, the largest serving as my office. The first floor features a living room, dining room and a kitchen split into two spaces, one original and the other a 1960s addition. To date, our contributions to the home's well-being have been replacing the roof and a warm-air heating system that spread like a giant octopus in the unfinished basement.

The walls of the basement, built with native fieldstone, make it naturally cool. Down there are a workshop and a laundry room with a window that offers a view of the outside wildlife at eye level. Some times of year I look up from the dryer to see a squirrel nibbling an acorn or the neighborhood black cat, paws on the sill, peering at me through luminous green eyes as if to say, "What are you up to?" Critters love our old yellow house. Rabbits scamper over the gravel drive. Birds chirp in a nest above the bathroom ceiling. Some years woodchucks nest under the porch.

In some ways our old house is charming with its old wavy leaded windows and front enclosed porch with wicker furniture. Tradesmen all drop off their names before they leave and say to call when we want to sell it. Realtors do likewise because our place is a rare opportunity for a young middle-class family to live in a community with terrific schools, a nature sanctuary and that glistening lake, still a popular spot. A five-minute walk gets a person to an old station that runs a train into Manhattan, and a ten-minute walk gets him to a quaint and vibrant downtown.

Yet from the moment my husband and I moved in we have received hundreds of messages, subliminal and direct, letting us know our home is "not enough." We have not demolished and rebuilt it, renovated or refurnished it, repainted or extended it. There is no central air conditioning or even window units. There is no garage, no automatic garbage disposal. Name an amenity. We don't have it. People have tried to embarrass, cajole, insist and otherwise pressure us into redoing the place. But it is exactly what we can afford and still have money, time and energy to pursue our arts, travel the country, support causes we love, volunteer in the community, and finance the good health and education of children in the United States and in faraway lands where the standard of living is so low that clean water sometimes is a challenge. We do all that and still eat well. We take walks. We talk to the animals. We're Thoreau people and, like him, believe the best house is the most unpretending, not the most picturesque, and that its cost is much more than its sale price. Its real cost includes the "life which is required to be exchanged for it, immediately or in the long run."

Don't get me wrong; we love wonderful homes. I have written about them for years. My husband designs them. We stay at darling bed-and-breakfasts whenever possible in our travels. But we appreciate homes in and of themselves. Not as symbols. The truth is, our house looks exactly like the standard of living we can afford. No more. And that makes people uncomfortable. They would rather see an ostentatious, or at least impressive, presentation, no matter the debt such would accrue or the life energy it would sap. Why? Because a house is more than a dwelling place in many parts of the United States. It is a statement of self-worth, a symbol of prosperity, a way of saying, "I have succeeded." But at what? A feat of architectural imagination or building ingenuity? Splendid. Building a home that blends with or defies its natural landscape is an accomplishment, depending on whether one admires Alvar Aalto or Le Corbusier. A feat of green design? Equally splendid. Photovoltaic windows, solar panels and geothermal energy systems are good for the planet. But in both those cases the triumph is in the artistry or the environmental conscience. Not the expense.

Indeed placing oneself in and around opulence can be a hindrance to living a life of value because affluence requires effort to maintain, leaving little or none for tending the house within, that small and specific place where we name who we are and discover the reason for our existence. True success resides in the realization we *are* the house of God. He dwells in us. Similarly, success does not require pursuing a thousand things and hoping one or two will suffice as a legacy. It is accepting the one task, the one theme, the one message, that is our divine inheritance, developing it (and ourselves) internally and manifesting it in the world in a thousand ways. Or ten thousand. Or one. Our achievements do not lead to success. They emanate from it.

Cumulating information, expectations, and material things for their own sake only obscures these realities. While true success does include some gathering, it is cumulation with a purpose. By and large, though, living a life of value is much more a matter of subtracting trappings and superfluities, affectations and delusions of grandeur until we are left only with the real riches: Silence, faith, God, the essence of who we are.

The daily harvest

How can we know when we are living a life of value?

When we get on with doing whatever makes our hearts lighter. When a sweet satisfaction is in the very air we breathe. When there is nowhere we would rather be than where we are in the moment, whether that be ministering to a dying person, writing a song, tending cattle or developing a vaccine. For years I had the privilege of working often with a photojournalist who loves images. Oh, how he adores them. He would sit, usually wordlessly, waiting for sunlight to wane or the right expression to cross a person's face. He would wait for symmetries to occur naturally and then capture them in a frame. One day he and I were at a farm where horses were nursed and rehabilitated. I was in the barn talking to the woman who ran the place. When she had to step away I stood at the barn door and, unbeknownst to the photographer, watched him work. He was down on one knee in a corral, steadily poised, observing a horse. He'd been out there for an hour. Suddenly the animal dropped to the dirt and rolled, and the photographer clicked and clicked as the dust flew. After the horse sprung back to its feet the photographer rested the camera on his lap, adjusted his baseball cap and sat back, a sloppy grin on his face. He was in his glory. He reveled in spending time with any life form for as long as it took to capture its essence.

His photographs are amazing. Given the opportunity, he would have stayed on that farm for weeks. Nothing would have broken his concentration or contentment. He shot prizefighters, geishas, births, riots, prayer services, Springsteen in concert, a woman in the process of being evicted, Wynton

Marsalis in concert, the aftermath of a hurricane, ball games. All with the same vision of fascination. Making pictures is his joy.

Though I can no longer recall the specifics, I once heard a famed writer being interviewed about his successes and failures during a very long career. When asked what kept him going, he paused and said, "I've been enchanted." Enchanted with discovering what works on the page. And, like me, enchanted every time by the prospect of making raw reality come alive in black and white. If there is difficulty and challenge—and there always is, thank God—both are safely embedded in an overarching love for the process itself.

In *Walden*, Thoreau captures the magical quality of this kind of success:

> *The true harvest of my daily life is somewhat as intangible and indescribable as the tints of morning or evening. It is a little star-dust caught, a segment of the rainbow which I have clutched.*

Some days the spirit of success, the bride of happiness, seems to favor us and some days not. How to keep the romance going? The key is in the condition of our minds. Do we allow our minds to be invaded, disturbed, distracted? But, we protest, life is complex and many duties assail us. It isn't every day that the sun shines and time is plentiful at the corral. True enough. Success is not sustained euphoria. It is fusing the self to a creative process, and giving it to that process, so as to recognize and use windows of opportunity when they open.

As to the good opinions, demands and distractions that surround us, success is not ignoring them but rather dealing with them wisely. Success leaves room for duty but is not the slave of every external demand that comes down the pike. Swami Dayananda once spoke to a huge audience on this point. Onstage he sat cross-legged on a white couch in front of a coffee table. On the table was a single orange flower in a vase. There being no other reference point, he picked up the blossom.

"If there is a flower, there is a flower and there is nothing you can do about it," he began. "You have no choice. You have no choice whatsoever."

There is no point in denying the flower exists, calling it something else or wishing it were something else. All those approaches are self-torment. The flower, like everything else in existence, must be honestly acknowledged for what it is. How?

"Keep the external external," the swami said. "Don't fall for words or accusations. Don't buy others' vibes. If someone disturbs you, they are inside you." Inside us are our loves and our affections, he explained, and our task is to ensure they remain undisturbed.

The swami addressed protecting the mind, but the sensei of a zendo I visited addressed the art of maintaining a peaceful mind. He pointed out the name of his sangha—Empty Bowl Zendo. The bowl, he said, is a metaphor for a person and the practice of zazen is a way to constantly clear out our bowls, our minds.

"An empty bowl is a perfect bowl," he said, "because it's ready for life. It's ready for whatever comes into it. We can receive everything."

The mind is a sacred stomping ground, both teachers tell us. Beware what we let in. Keep it current and orderly. The alternative is living in a state of cacophonous irrelevant overload and eventually losing the ability to hear the voice of our own soul, the only voice from which we can learn our true value.

One of the most content and successful people I've met was known as "Nanna." She lived next door to me when I was growing up. She was 90 when I met her. She lived with her daughter and son-in-law and still worked the job she'd had for decades. Nanna tended the grounds at a cemetery not a mile from our street. She was good friends with the morning sun and walked to her early shift at the graveyard until she hit her mid-90s. Then she got a ride.

As a kid I thought of her job as gruesome and could not imagine spending even one whole hour in the company of the dead. Wasn't she depressed? Maybe, I reasoned in my little girl brain, Nanna could not get a better job. But then there was the reality she was still doing it long past the age of retirement because, of all things, she liked it. Nanna was an enigma. I hardly ever saw her without a smile on her face, her eyes sparkling through her silver granny glasses, whether she was limping down the street or sitting by her daughter's pool bathing her aged, wrinkled, sagging body in the sun. If she were self-conscious, especially since she often sunbathed next to her long-legged, smooth-skinned bronzed beauty of a 20-year-old grand-daughter, she never showed it.

Nanna was childlike in her pleasures. She let watermelon juice drip down her chin. She liked sitting outside until night fell, not surrendering to sleep until cricket song pervaded the trees that canopied the back yard of her daughter's property. The neighborhood knew when she finally retired for the night by the sound of the screen door loudly snapping shut behind her.

Everyone said she had magical hands when it came to the vines, flowers and vegetables in her private garden, and so it seemed when she came to our front door from time to time, offering us fresh tomatoes and zucchini she carried by holding up her long black skirt on either side. Nanna rarely uttered sentences or words, though she was fully capable of doing so. She seemed to prefer sounds — the "um-um" when she tasted something scrumptious, the "he-he" of a light moment, the "bah!" she used to banish some annoyance. In my midlife, long after her death, I wonder how she conducted herself in the cemetery day after day, weeding the plantings around the graves, seeing that the shrubs along the periphery were perfectly in alignment, knowing what to plant where and when so there always would be colorful beauty in that final resting place. Maybe she talked to the dead. Maybe she did not talk and her presence was her communion with life.

By the measure of the swami and the sensei, Nanna was a success. She knew her mind and protected its sanctity. She spent no time analyzing or second-guessing. Her example speaks to me now: To live a life of value we needn't impress, strive or seek. All we need to do is emerge.

Stories come and stories go

Letting go

For ten years an earthen bowl whose rounded bottom fit perfectly in my two cupped hands never was far from my sight. First it sat on the lower level of my nightstand and then on a table in my office. In the months after Victoria Helen was stillborn the fertility bowl had been gifted to me. I liked its gooselike neck and that it opened on top. The opening, I fancied, represented the place the breath of divine life would enter the bowl, would enter me again. How wonderful, I thought at the time, to have a physical object to artfully hold such a promising energy. Perhaps there would be another opportunity for me to deliver a baby over the threshold of danger and into the world and a long, healthy life. My next child, I dreamed, would open her eyes and let out a wail that meant she drew a breath. By God, actually breathed!

The bowl was the color of the American Southwest—sand, copper and black. Around its circumference were painted several figures of Kokopelli, the hunchbacked, flute-playing, ever-dancing casanova of a fertility god whose image Bill and I enjoyed finding everywhere we looked during the summer we went to Taos. We remembered that land of pink/orange sunsets and adobe homes so fondly. There was the big pueblo, the End of the Universe Café and the smell of sagebrush and ponderosa pine, the latter so much like homemade vanilla ice cream. Kokopellis are ubiquitous among the ancient petroglyphs painted and carved on the rock walls and boulders of New Mexico. In native mythology Kokopelli enjoys a special role in human affairs. He carries seeds and songs on his back, which explains the hump, and it is said that a woman who hears his flute soon will discover she is pregnant. (My husband liked Kokopelli just because he is a musician.) That summer, four years before Victoria was conceived, we'd bought a set of metal Kokopelli Christmas ornaments to hang on our Douglas fir. This deity always was welcome in our house and it was comforting, even after Victoria's death, to see him again.

But, as this story goes, Kokopelli was unable to work his magic. I never again became pregnant. Still, whenever Bill and I returned home from numerous orientation sessions at adoption agencies, there was Kokopelli on the bowl playing, dancing, holding out hope. By 2003 I knew I would not raise a child. But I never removed the bowl. By late 2008 I realized the sight of the dancing around its circumference stirred feelings of sadness and disappointment. Not even Kokopelli, whose charming tunes and fertile seeds had worked for centuries, could produce for me.

Around my fiftieth birthday in January 2009 an ordained Taoist minister invited Bill and me to a Chinese New Year party—a first for us.

"Bring something that symbolizes an energy you want to let go so you can be free to embrace a new one," she said. I pondered her instruction during the drive home. As I entered my home office and let my briefcase fall off my shoulder, my gaze caught the bowl. Whose hope was it holding now, that of an ever-expectant woman whose dream never realized? Did that woman exist anymore? I had lived through the story of the stillbirth of my daughter and I had lived through the story of healing from it. Yet I had kept the bowl not only in my office but at eye level so that I saw it whenever I looked up from my writing. Symbols are powerful physical representations of spirit. I wondered what that power does when it lingers after its day is spent.

Bowl in hand, I went to the Chinese New Year party. Tables of food lined the back of the huge room and people sat or stood in a semicircle, several rows deep, facing the front. Mei Jin had created a clear space there, except for two large cardboard boxes. One by one, individuals came forward, some holding an object, most with a folded piece of paper on which they had written a description of the energy they wanted to release from their lives. I approached with the bowl. Mei Jin told me to hold its energy in my thoughts and then toss it into the box, letting it go with a loud and hearty "Ah!" to hasten and intensify the energy's release. I cradled the bowl, as I had so many times, in both hands, and dropped it into a box. It landed gently on a thick bed of folded papers.

"No," the Taoist said. "To release its energy, the bowl must shatter." She reached into the box, picked up the bowl, made an opening in the layers of papers, and with a surprisingly loud and long "Ahahahahah!" lifted my bowl high over her head before hurling it with such force that it hit the bottom of the box and the hard floor and shattered. I walked back to my place near the food tables.

After the last person had finished, a large gong from China was wheeled into the room and placed between the two boxes. All of us were instructed to close our eyes. The sounding of the gong would help send all the outgrown energies from the room. The sheer power of the first gong overtook me; I felt as if I were inside the sound and held a nearby table for stability. The second gong astonished me. In my third eye I saw an ethereal image of myself ten years earlier, the year Victoria had died, fly out of the box, through a wall of the room and into the heavens. This former self looked over her shoulder and smiled serenely at me before disappearing, like a shooting star, across the night sky of my consciousness. She was leaving, really leaving. A tear rolled down my cheek as I silently mouthed, "Thank you." By the third gong—a sound that surely seems to emanate from another dimension—a heaviness left my body. I wiped the tear.

That version of myself took so much with her when she left, as I would learn in the months afterward. She took a tentativeness about life, thin as a veil, that I always had had to push aside. She took a sense of sorrowful defeat that used to singe the edges of my consciousness though never burned or damaged it. Mostly, though, she flew off with a certain deference that had at times left me voiceless; I always had words to express what I felt but at times not the power to utter them. Before these qualities of consciousness left me, I could not have named or explained them to anyone, including myself.

The minister called a week later. "That was some healing," she said. "It will last forever."

At times I have asked myself if my spiritual odyssey is that of a homeless person. I started out in the Catholic church and then traveled among schools of thought and belief, curious about what they shared and how they differed. Was I appropriating—not just appreciating—other cultures and ideas? After the Chinese New Year ceremony I realized I have not been homeless. I *am* my own temple. Each exploration has not been a wayward step or a stroll down others' paths. Rather I have been heading toward the center of my heart and doing no more or less than following my God-given instincts.

The same natural enthusiasm that propeled me into journalism—the telling of hundreds of stories from as many viewpoints—drives me into philosophies and spiritualities of all colors and varieties. Faith is not holding immutable beliefs but being willing to challenge and redraw them, all the while trusting every brushstroke of the human experience is painted on a divine canvas.

We are not meant to live out the identity we inherit by birthright—or any one we are easily offered—unless we decide it suits us and consciously choose to do so. We are designed for movement and growth. In exploring the boundaries of our circumstances, we come to know how we are limitless, how we are not and the knowledge to distinguish between the two. The knowledge is key. Without it we may bypass the understanding that we are filled with God and land on the grave and dangerous misunderstanding that we are God. That was Aristotle's definition of a tragedy: When we act like gods, we do ourselves in.

But we do have divine qualities of discernment that help us wisely direct our fates. Only those qualities can steer us clear of disaster. They help the battered wife to pack her bags and leave and the alcoholic to put down the drink. They help the mistress resist the tryst and the employee with the overbearing boss summon the courage to exercise some self-respecting option.

In a bookstore café one day I read Jean Anouilh's *Antigone* (whose very name means "unbending"), a one-act play about the daughter of Oedipus who suffered a classically tragic death as a victim of circumstances she set in motion. As I read, a woman sat down next to me with two colorful books. She poured over them while sipping a frozen chocolate drink, as if the books were part of the luscious dessert. She lifted her head once and said this was her free time in the week. Not wanting to miss another moment of freedom, she returned to reading. When she left I reached over and looked at the covers of the books she left behind: *The Creative License: Giving Yourself Permission to be the Artist You Truly Are* and *You Can Heal Your Life*.

Her soul had stirred and her mind was helping her birth a new self.

When any of us comes to the knowledge we need not hold onto identities and misconceptions that ultimately will kill us one way or the other — and then act on the knowledge — we have escaped a needlessly painful fate. Every life contains necessary pain. Why invite needless pain, too? The divine power in each of us is not about commanding subservience or exerting our will to the exclusion of all other wills. Those are perversions. Rather, it is about our power to change ourselves, to adapt, to dream anew, to not become tragically stuck in any one version of the self.

The problem with living inside one story — even a pleasant or productive one — is that the longer we stay, the more we overidentify with that one way of being at the expense of others. Who is the businessman who blazes trails and creates empires when he steps out of the entrepreneurial arena and into retirement? The Olympian athlete when he no longer competes in elite circles? A victim after he surmounts the injustices levied against him? Essential growing vehicles that they are, stories are not intended to be impermeable shells that trap us. They are more like the elastic membranes of eggs. We are supposed to grow inside them before cracking them open and re-emerging, transformed and ready to write a new story. The changing of the story is what distinguishes human life from all other life on the planet.

Consider grief, disappointment or hardship at first strong enough to flood our senses, emotions, thoughts and body. These forces engulf us and present us with a choice: Stay inside them, or grow ourselves — or, more precisely, our spiritual core — until we become large enough to contain the grief, disappointment or hardship. If we stay inside circumstances, they become our master. If we outgrow and shed them, they become our teacher and we the wise students. Thoreau did not live at his idyllic Walden Pond his whole life. He left after two years because he had accomplished the objective he set for himself, namely, to distinguish what is essential in life from what is superfluous:

> I left the woods for as good a reason as I went there. Perhaps it seemed to me that I had several more lives to live, and could not spare any more time for that one.

The challenge of spiritual living is to keep evolving ourselves through stories in such a way that allows God to shine ever more brightly through our personhood, to remain open to the ever-cascading inner divine healing force.

This idea echoes through time and the natural world. Everything, including us, is in motion. Consult the Theory of Relativity. Or the Principle of Vibration in *The Kybalion*. Our very health is dependent on the flow of chi throughout the body, as stated in *The Yellow Emperor's Classic of Internal Medicine*. The challenge is in staying so aware of the divine within us that we feel a constant cleansing of our minds, our outlooks, our very cells. Rumi knew this as he wrote, "When you do things from your soul, you feel a river moving in you, a joy."

In Fallingwater

Famed architect Frank Lloyd Wright was raised amid the fields and streams of rural Wisconsin where he surely saw humans as part of a gigantic natural splendor. He designed homes so integrated with their surroundings that the structures became an organic piece of the landscapes in which they were set. Not the least of these is Fallingwater in Pennsylvania, a summer retreat home designed by Wright in the 1930s for the Kaufmann family of Pittsburgh, known for their department store dynasty. The home, now a national historic landmark, is built atop a waterfall in the Allegheny Mountains. The stone for its walls were quarried nearby. Its ochre concrete cantilevered terraces jut out horizontally from the rockface, and one interior staircase actually leads to and ends in an active stream that flows below the home.

The day I stood on the balcony off the living room, holding an umbrella, rain fell in sheets from the sky, rolled off the cantilevered terraces around me and cascaded from the falls below my feet. Meanwhile, the rushing sound of the stream below, usually a tinkling musical presence, crescendoed into a watery symphony. I had to remind myself that even the human body is seventy-five percent water. What transcendence to stand in the middle of this natural theater which demonstrated so vividly the dynamics always at work in and around us. We and the world appear solid and static but nothing could be further from true.

When I looked down at the falls I saw rendered the most exquisite spiritual memoir ever. I saw the moving waters of spirit flow over and between the rocky dramas of human life. No use trying to blast the rocks out of existence. No sense trying to move or defy them. Instead Wright designed a house that included the rocks and the water; he made art of their inevitable meeting. He could have found a flat easy surface on which to build, but then the house would not have told the story of life, and there is no doubt Fallingwater, with its amazing juxtaposition-ing of life forces, talks to every one who walks through it. It is spiritual genius. No doubt engineers, artists and doctors who walked through the house that day were absorbing all kinds of insights about structures, shapes and anatomy. But Fallingwater showed me that what appears to be a storm falling upon us can, when seen from a different angle, actually be a tide that elevates and moves us into our next phases and narratives, hopes, and emotions.

Standing inside Fallingwater is standing inside the mind of Frank Lloyd Wright. Yes, the waters of spirit rain down and through us but the inspirations can be no more than runoff or stagnant pools in a mind that does nothing with them. The goal of being human is to order the mind in such a way as to make the most of the life-giving flow — to channel and direct it, as Fallingwater does. This is how we make meaning. This is how we change. We choose to pay such close attention to our own inner states and surroundings that we ask: What has left? What has just arrived? How can I make this better? How can I make this more beautiful? Then we take an action and what follows is a mini-version of the creation of the universe, of the time in the *Book of Genesis* when God said, "Let there be light" and in so doing brought a new order into the cosmic void.

In Frank Lloyd Wright's house I saw how this process was at work in the vast grief in which I was floating after Victoria's death. Everything I thought I knew, and all my expectations, shattered into free-floating pieces. I stayed still until my divine core uttered, *This has meaning.* Then my mind asked, *What is the meaning? How can I heal myself? How can I make this better for all of us?* And so healing began with a divine stirring. The mind took up the message and focused its attention. Its walls and cantilevers welcomed the flow of spirit until I no longer was drowning in a stagnant ocean of existential disappointment, painful memories and broken dreams. Then that spirit flowed out my fingers and onto the page.

Healing, then, is a process built into the human machinery. No matter the decimated landscapes in which we find ourselves, we need only let the divine currents flow over them. There comes a time the decimation itself is the past and the flowing is the present and the present is the headwater of the future.

In his book *Finding Flow: The Psychology of Engagement with Everyday Life*, psychologist and author Mihaly Csikszentmihalyi suggests that the quality of now determines the quality of the future:

A person who grows up experiencing most of the day as neither important nor enjoyable is unlikely to find much meaning in the future.

Csikszentmihalyi also proposes a new myth for the twenty-first century, one built on the scientific understandings of matter and energy which make it clear that organisms, including us, evolve toward a greater complexity. In a less sophisticated world, he contends, a non-conformist view may be considered a heresy, or at least wrong. But now different views may rightly be attributed to a different angle of vision or scale of observation. In such a world even very old concepts of good and evil can change. Good can be the word used to describe a flowing active mind that can overcome inertia and take into account complex factors, including the future and the well-being of others. In the new myth, evil can be a word used to describe the state of entropy to which the mind defaults when it does not order and renew itself. This type of mind, much less able to account for complexity, more readily allows itself to be usurped or overwhelmed.

Heaven is flow, those moments "when heart, will, and mind are on the same page," according to Cziksentmihalyi. His new hell includes a provocative interpretation of the devil:

> Hell in this scenario is simply the separation of the individual from the flow of life. It is clinging to the past, to the self, to the safety of inertia. There is a trace of this sense in the root of the word for "devil": it comes from the Greek dia bollein, to separate or break asunder. What is diabolical is to weaken the emerging complexity by withdrawing one's psychic energy from it.

Heaven and hell are not concepts set in stone. They are among the most elastic and complex of ideas, and that is a very good thing to say out loud. The explication that author Elizabeth Gilbert finds in Indonesia is among the most intriguing I've encountered. In *Eat Pray Love*, she writes of a conversation she had with a Balinese medicine man who describes meditations in which he ascends seven layers up to heaven and seven layers down to hell. The latter, he tells Gilbert, is more dangerous and not for beginners. When she asks what hell is like, he answers, "Same like heaven." The universe is a circle, he says, so all paths — up or down — lead to love.

We certainly live in a complex world. It has teemed with diversity and alternate viewpoints even before our understandings of matter and energy. How much more healthy for us to experiment with alternate forms of the myths on which we were raised, than to stay obediently inside one even long after it has squelched our development and vitality.

With his psychological bent, Czikszentmihalyi does not delve into theological ideas of God or spirit, though he makes room for them in some people's experiences. At the heart of his work, though, is the essential notion that everything, including knowledge, including his new myth, is always evolving.

Of all our life journeys, the one we take inward is the most important. Here in the twenty-first century we stand at a spot on the eternal spectrum of belief that, like all others before it, deserves its own testaments and articulations. Unlike other ages, ours is pervaded by technology, which has helped faith and belief blend into unprecedented mosaics. How incomprehensible it would have been, just a century ago, for a Catholic man to be the sensei of a zendo in an Episcopal church or for a Jewish cancer patient to practice yoga as part of treatment. Yet this is our world.

The mosaic affects all our spiritual lives and begs to be added to, grown, pruned and corrected as we go. Faith is no longer something just received, though receipt is important. It can be born in Scripture—yours and mine and his and theirs—but it grows in the heart, the mind and the unfolding of life. Faith is something to be engaged and matured.

All the more reason for each of us to take the journey to our divine centers. For it is our consciousness that keeps the eternal flame well tended there. Or extinguishes it.

About the Author

Lorraine Ash, M.A., is an author, journalist, and essayist as well as a writing teacher. *Self and Soul: On Creating a Meaningful Life* is her second book.

Karen Mancinelli Photography / www.kmpIMAGES.com

Her first memoir, *Life Touches Life: A Mother's Story of Stillbirth and Healing*, was published by NewSage Press and has circulated throughout the United States as well as in the Middle East, Australia, Europe, China, Canada, and Mexico.

Shorter memoiric works have appeared in anthologies, including *Steeped in the World of Tea*, and various journals and webzines such as *Cairn*, *Journeys*, *Ducts*, and *Recovering the Self: A Journal of Hope and Healing*.

Lorraine also is a veteran journalist whose feature articles and series have won seventeen national, state, and regional awards and have appeared in daily newspapers across the country. She has been an editor/reporter since 1982, currently for New Jersey Press Media, a Gannett newspaper group.

In her workshops and writing retreats Lorraine fuses rigorous original literary techniques with a wide range of spiritual, psychological, and philosophical thought. Participants learn to find their strongest writing voice, structure their stories in compelling ways, and see their lives from surprising and useful new angles.

Lorraine belongs to the Story Circle Network, Association of Writers and Writing Programs, and Investigative Reporters and Editors.

She lives in New Jersey with her husband, Bill.

Lorraine is available in person or through Skype for book clubs and other groups interested in discussing *Self and Soul: On Creating a Meaningful Life* and how writing helps people to understand and direct their inner and outer lives throughout the life cycle.

Contact Lorraine through:

www.LorraineAsh.com

 or

www.CapeHouseBooks.com

52094872R00106

Made in the USA
Middletown, DE
16 November 2017